RECLAIMING INACTIVE CHURCH MEMBERS

Mark S. Jones

BROADMAN PRESS
Nashville, Tennessee

Scripture quotations are from the King James Version of the Bible.

Scripture quotations marked NKJV are from the *New King James Version*. Copyright © 1979, 1980, 1982, Thomas Nelson, Inc., Publishers.

Scripture quotations marked NEB are from *The New English Bible*. Copyright © The Delegates of the Oxford University Press and the Syndics of the Cambridge University Press, 1961, 1970. Reprinted by permission.

© Copyright 1988 • Broadman Press

All rights reserved

4232-42

ISBN: 0-8054-3242-6

Dewey Decimal Classification: 254.5

Subject Heading: CHURCH MEMBERSHIP

Library of Congress Catalog Card Number: 87-32075

Printed in the United States of America

To
Marlene and Carli
who keep me active

Preface

One response to the church growth movement has been a concern about the ministerial side of churchmanship. Deliberate as well as unconscious decrease of certain ministries has occurred in the wake of the growth emphasis. In some ways, church work has been reduced to a science and mere methodology with its own supporting research and analysis base. While many proponents of the movement propose to provide a limited perspective on ecclesiology, admitting up front the narrowness of their field, it does not appear that the typical church worker understands these limitations. The appeal of results has been very strong, too often drowning out the cries of other ministries not yielding such immediate and tangible success.

As a pastor, with a burden for evangelism and discipleship, I support and appreciate the contributions of those who have taught us many practical principles for growing churches. I have also found myself wrestling with the flip side: the needs in the church that cannot be addressed by church growth principles but require pastoral care, such as counseling and social ministries. It is not an either-or proposition. It is churches reaching and teaching people and also binding their wounds.

On the rolls of churches are the names of persons who have been saved and lost—saved by Christ and lost to the church. They have been evangelized but have somehow forgotten the Good News. They are ignored and relegated to the dark corners. The reasons for the existence of these ecclesiastical isolation wards are many and the experiences varied, but the issue is widespread. This book, therefore, is from the heart of a pastor who wishes to see the churches of our Lord reach out with both arms: the arm of evangelism and the arm of loving fellowship. With such a ministerial approach, churches should see more souls cured of their spiritual ills and indeed more results from outreach efforts.

The illustrations in this book are provided to allow for greater understanding of the material. It has been difficult to provide illustrations that realistically depict the principles presented while maintaining the anonymity of the persons involved. Purely fictional examples would not allow for illustrations with integrity while factual accounts could depict persons in such a way as may be libelous. The solution was to alter factual situations and combine fragments of these situations to create a new and unique fictional illustration.

Although the illustrations may contain fragments of actual situations, the author has been careful to piece these fragments together in such a fashion as to disallow any recognition of the actual situation. Names and locations have been altered. Even the nature of the situations have been changed significantly. There are some illustrations, such as of a certain church, which are purely fictional. These illustrations are provided as a way of depicting hypothetically what could be if the principles illustrated were employed.

Any similarlity of the illustrations provided in this book with real or imagined situations on the part of the reader is purely coincidental.

The author is indebted to many for their gracious and valuable help in the process of developing the understanding that led to the eventual production of this book as well as those who assisted in the actual writing of the manuscript. Bill Tillman and Preston Bright gave competent guidance and input in the research and ministry project which formed the basis of the book. A special thanks to Bill for his editorial help in the initial stages of the manuscript and for his encouragement in seeking publication.

Contents

Introduction

A Growing Problem

Pastor Jones sat in his study looking at the latest church pictorial directory. He called out to his secretary, "Who are all these people?" Faith Church's pastor of a year's tenure could not recognize many of the faces in the directory. Loss of memory was not the problem. Rather, Jones shared this plight and concern with multitudes of ministers and laymen.

Many members never darken the door of their church. Their names remain on church rolls like inscriptions on tombstones in a country cemetery, forgotten and unknown. A recent study revealed that 29 percent of resident members of Southern Baptist churches are inactive. A majority of pastors consider this a problem of serious to crucial proportions.[1]

John Savage, in his study of the United Methodist Church, found that nearly 33 percent of each congregation's membership was in the inactive category.[2] A Gallup Poll revealed the following information about American adults, eighteen years of age and over:

Church members	68%	102 million
Active members	56%	84 million
Attend church regularly	42%	63 million
Born again	34%	51 million[3]

It is interesting that 14 percent of American adults consider themselves to be active members of a church yet not attend regularly! If regular church attendance is an indication of activity, then according to these figures, 38 percent of adult church members in this country are inactive!

"How could this be?" Jones continued as he emerged from his office. "Our church is barely five years old and so many of our members never attend!" Pastor Jones did not know it, but this trend is characteristic of most churches. When a church reaches its fifth birthday, it has usually seen its most aggressive period of numerical growth.[4] As the years pass, so lengthens the list of church members. New families join the congregation and are incorporated into the life and ministry of the church. Unnoticed, many of these members slip out the proverbial back door and are never seen again. Soon the number of silent absent members mounts to a sizeable portion of the membership.

Attitude Adjustment

In 1867, a forward-looking secretary of state, William H. Seward, led the nation to purchase the territory of Alaska. In exchange, the Russians got $7,200,000 in gold. The action was widely ridiculed as "Seward's Frog Pond," "Seward's Folly," and "590,000 square miles of icebergs and polar bears." What seemed to some a foolish investment turned out to be a literal gold mine. The wealth of Alaska's natural resources has repaid the purchase price several times over.

People often think of inactive members as a group of delinquent backsliders who should be written off the church rolls. For them the inactive membership roster represents a barren wasteland of unresponsiveness. Others, however, see a fertile field for ministry.

Your attitude about inactivity depends upon your motivations. It's not just how you define inactivity but why. We all have reasons for labeling and categorizing people. We call a politician a liberal or conservative depending on our views about government policy. Likewise, the perception church leaders have of inactive members is linked to the actions they intend to take about inactivity. If all you want to do is to cut the drop-outs from the rolls, you will look at inactivity differently from someone who wants to reach out to these straying members and minister to them.

What is an inactive member to you? A sampling of the constitutions and bylaws of churches demonstrates that little unanimity exists concerning the precise nature of inactivity. Some churches choose not to make such a determination. Other congregations are very strict in their church discipline.

The purpose of this book is to equip concerned persons to minister to the inactive members of their church. Why are you interested in inactive members? How do you define inactivity? Write down your definition. (That's right, lay this book down and write it out.)

Now, look at your definition. Did you define inactivity in terms of time and behavior or in terms of a process? Was your description something like "a member who hasn't attended or contributed in the last six months"? If so, your emphasis is on time (six months) and behavior (attended and contributed). On the other hand, did your definition sound like "a member who has dropped out of the church"? Then you are thinking in terms of a process (dropped out).

Which is the right way to define inactivity? Actually, its both! Inactivity certainly has a lot to do with attendance and financial support over a period of time. But, it also involves a process—the process of becoming inactive.

Time and behavior are only relative indicators of inactivity. Some members attend three times a week; others only once. Some members tithe; some do not. Some members give money to the church every week; some give faithfully once a month. A definition of inactivity must go beyond just time and behavior; it must describe activity (and inactivity) as a process. Members are constantly becoming more or less active. An inactive member is someone in the process of becoming less active. This process may take one day or one year.

Why do you define inactivity the way you do? What is motivating you? Is your inclination toward church discipline and maintaining a "clean" membership roll? Then you probably will define inactivity in purely measurable terms, such as time and behavior. If your motivation is to minister to the inactive members of your church, your definition will reflect this. Inactivity is a painful process that hurting people are going through—not just numbers and percentages.

When I was in elementary school, we had the "new math." Mom and Dad had trouble figuring it out. It was different. I've recently discovered an even newer math. I call it "growth math." You find growth math used at almost any pastors' conference, staff meeting, Sunday School workers meeting, and even in casual conversation. Just ask a pastor, staff member, Bible study leader, or deacon what the church or group is running in Sunday School attendance. Let's say the attendance ranges from seventy to ninety. While conventional math might compute the average at eighty, growth math figures it a ninety!

The optimism of growth math is commendable. Numbers are important for they represent precious souls. But, growth for numbers' sake is a travesty of ministry! Church work can all too easily get sidetracked by a spirit of competitiveness. Too often success in church work is seen only as numerical and material gain.

Are you playing the numbers game or doing ministry? The first rule of the numbers game is to make your situation look as good as possible. Those who are caught up in the success model are usually expert players in the numbers game. Their concept of church is bound up in statistics and analyses. Satisfaction comes only with great numerical strides. It sounds impressive if you can say you had 75 percent of your Sunday School enrollment present last Sunday. But, how many people had to be dropped from the roll to get that statistic?

What is the church here for? Your answer to that question reflects whether you are following the success model or the ministry model in doing church. The ministry model teaches us that "the Son of Man did not come to be served but to serve" (Mark 10:45, NEB). Christian ministry is addressing the needs of persons in the name and love of Jesus Christ. Christ may not be as interested in our numbers as in what we're doing for the persons those numbers represent.

"Where were the hearing?"

Paul describes the church as a body. Each member has a unique function.

For the body is not one member, but many. If the foot shall say, Because I am not the hand, I am not of the body; is it therefore not of the body? And if the ear shall say, Because I am not the eye, I am not of the body; is it therefore not of the body? If the whole body were an eye, where were the hearing? If the whole were hearing, where were the smelling? But now hath God set the members every one of them in the body, as it hath pleased him (1 Cor. 12:14-18).

A vital church ministry accommodates this uniqueness in its members. In addition, the unique needs of persons, such as those who are inactive, are recognized.

A variety of approaches has been tried in reclaiming inactive members, with varied success. Pastors report that most of these efforts at reclamation are ineffective.[5]

Why don't these common approaches work? Maybe we do not know how to listen well. Of those churches providing training programs for member reclamation, most emphasize visiting skills. Approaches with proven effectiveness stress understanding and the development of listening skills. In the case of reclamation ministry, the church needs to be "all ears"!

The approaches outlined in this book grew out of reclamation ministry in my pastoral experience. An emphasis on reclaiming inactive members in my pastorate resulted in a 256% increase in attendance on the part of these members. This statistic can in no way reflect the long-term effect. It is gratifying to see members revitalized back into the life and fellowship of the church. Many of our active members are testimonies to the effectiveness of caring concern. The sensitive ministry of their brethren helped restore waning commitments. By utilizing the principles set forth in this book, you can have a significant ministry to those unseen members of your church!

This book is written as a workbook. As you read through the text you will be asked to stop and think about practical applications. At the end of each chapter are instructions for implementing your own program of ministry to inactive members. To get you started, the first set of instructions follow. Go to work!

Application

1. Did you write out your definition of inactivity? Revise that definition. Does your definition provide a way of measuring activity? If you were on a committee to write or revise your church's constitution and bylaws, how would you define active and inactive membership? Include a time frame (three months, one year, etc.). What are the behaviors of an inactive member? Attendance? Contributions? Also, be sure your definition entails the process of becoming inactive (trends, a point of departure, etc.).

2. Write one paragraph explaining why you are interested in reclaiming inactive members.

3. List actions you and/or your church are currently doing to reach out to inactive members? Are these actions effective in your estimation? How could they be made more effective?

Notes

[1]Lewis Wingo, *Inactive Member Survey,* The Sunday School Board of the Southern Baptist Convention, Nashville, TN 37234, July 1985. Used by permission.

[2]John S. Savage, *The Apathetic and Bored Church Member* (Pittsford: LEAD Consultants, Inc., 1976), p. 13.

[3]As quoted in C. Peter Wagner, *Your Church Can Be Healthy,* (Nashville: Abingdon Press, 1982), pp. 102-103.

[4]Statistics of Southern Baptist churches, 1980-1983 indicates that the ratios for baptisms to resident members, Sunday School attendance, and per church for new churches was significantly higher than for established churches, thus a higher rate of growth for new churches over older churches.

[5]Wingo. Of the various approaches taken to reclamation, very few pastors reported these to be "very effective."

I
Why Are Members Inactive?

A crew from Ace Moving Company wrestled an antique upright piano down three flights of stairs and into the lobby of the apartment building. One discouraging fact became obvious. In planning his strategy for the removal of the bulky instrument, the foreman had made one simple mistake. The door was not large enough! Obviously the piano had been moved into the building through the front door. It was assumed that the piano could be moved out of the building through the same door. What the foreman did not know was that the front door had been replaced with a slightly narrower one during a recent remodeling. What a difference an inch makes!

What does moving pianos have to do with reclaiming inactive members? For starters, members do not always leave by the same "door" they came in. Their reasons for becoming active in a church are not always related to their reasons for becoming inactive. Secondly, before embarking upon a task as monumental as moving a piano—or seeking to reclaim the inactive members of your church—be sure to check out your presuppositions. Else, you do a lot of work for nothing.

Let's look at one of my presuppositions about reclamation. *Ministry to inactive members must begin with discovering their needs.* Conversely, trying to get inactive members active again without addressing their needs is a waste of time—yours and theirs. It just won't work.

In this section of the book, we are going to explore the various dimensions of inactivity. The definable stages of inactivity are discussed in chapter 1. An overview of why members become inactive initially is presented. In chapters 2, 3, and 4, the psychological, spiritual, and sociological dimensions of inactivity is documented.

1
The Process of Inactivity

Many "shade tree" mechanical ventures have been attempted on my old car. It is very difficult, if not impossible, to fix something until you know where it is broken. I've also learned that the quick-fix additives sold in auto parts stores seldom work in repairing engine problems. Normally, a significant expense of time, energy, and money is required to get a broken-down car running again.

Likewise, there are no short cuts to reclaiming inactive members. If you're not willing to invest time and energy, your success at reclamation will be limited. This ministry also requires a compassionate willingness to make yourself vulnerable to share the pain others are experiencing.

Any person interested in reclaiming inactive members must understand why members become inactive in the first place. I have the greatest respect for my family doctor. Once I thought I had the flu. I had nausea and all the symptoms of the flu. I kept telling myself I had the flu. A week went by, then two weeks. Still nauseous. Finally, I went to the doc. He poked around on my stomach and said, "I think you have an intestinal virus." Great. He put me on a very strict diet (practically nothing). I was given some pills for the nausea and told to call him in a couple of days. I didn't get better in spite of the starvation routine. Back in the office, the doctor poked around some more. "I think you might have an ulcer," he said. Tests were scheduled. Sure enough, I had an ulcer. After a couple of months on a proper diet (of semi-real food) and medication, I recovered completely.

Why do I have such respect for my doctor? He knows the difference between symptoms and causes. Had he not known the difference, I might still be taking nausea medicine, starving to death, and nursing an ulcer.

What are the symptoms of inactivity? Inactivity! When members quit being active they are probably becoming inactive. But, why are they becoming inactive? It does little good to treat the symptoms until you know the causes.

Often inactive members know their symptoms but are unaware of the causes of their inactivity. The symptoms are what they tell you—their reasons or explanations for being less active. But the real need may be under the surface. You may have to do a little poking around before you get at the real reasons for members' inactivity.

There is a profound difference between *surface reasons* (symptoms) and *root causes* of inactivity. The distinction was not clear to me at first. I began to notice that a problem that caused one person to become less active might not affect someone else. A chronic ailment may sideline one member. Another member with a similar difficulty would remain very faithful in attendance. There was something deeper under the surface that was causing the inactivity.

What are the reasons for and the underlying processes which cause inactivity? The two are often hard to distinguish. This chapter will help you to sort it all out.

Categories of Inactivity

A pastor was visiting an inactive member one day. "Why is it," he pleaded, "that you never come to church anymore?" "Well," responded the parishioner, "it's on account of that oak tree in my front yard." "What's that oak tree got to do with it?" queried the minister. "I suppose one excuse is as good as another," came the reply.

If you are going to ascertain the reason why a member is inactive, you must look beyond casual excuses. Often, members will not share real reasons for their inactivity until you've earned the right to be trusted. Otherwise, one excuse is as good as another. Excuses are a means of getting someone off your back. Until you convince the member that you truly are interested in him, excuses are probably all you will hear.

Excuses may also be a way for the inactive member to hide the real reasons for his inactivity from himself. The member is avoiding the issue. Progress comes only when the member accepts responsibility for his inactivity.

You will probably find that reasons for inactivity fit into one of four categories: *conflict, unmet expectations, lack of affinity,* or an *inability to relate.* As we discuss these categories, see if you can find any familiar faces.

Conflict

Conflict is by far the most encompassing category of inactivity. As many as 50 percent of inactive members may fall into this category![1] Lyle Schaller pointed to conflict as a crucial issue for churches.

> On a given day in perhaps three-quarters of all churches the ministry of that congregation is reduced significantly as a result of nonproductive conflict. In perhaps one-fourth of all churches that internal conflict is so sufficiently severe that it must be reduced before the parish can redirect its energies and resources toward formulating new goals and expanding its ministry.[2]

Conflict in the local church is virtually unavoidable. Many persons are very uncomfortable around conflict. This virtual instinct for avoiding conflict plays a role in members becoming inactive.

The direction and focus of conflict may vary. The pastor may become the focal point of conflict. He is perhaps the most visible and representative member of the church. As such, the pastor is put in the limelight of conflict in many situations. This becomes obvious when a church calls a new pastor. Members who joined the church under the previous pastor's ministry may have difficulty adjusting to and accepting the new minister. He is not like Brother Smith, they will say. In other words, he lacks those qualities and personality traits they admired in his predecessor.

Churches must realize that the pastor cannot be made the scapegoat for every problem that arises. If we are to have consistent, loving fellowship in our congregations, conflict must be dealt with honestly. Often the problems blamed on a new or previous pastor are deeply rooted in the interpersonal relationships of members.

Certainly members may have bona fide conflicts with their pastor. Differences of opinion or emphases, doctrinal issues, or personal tiffs may lead to disharmony between member and pastor. Such conflicts take on possibly huge proportions in the eyes of the member. The pastor is a significant personality in the church. Members seldom will remain active in a church wherein they feel tension with the pastor.

The significance of the pastor's personality is demonstrated every Sunday. Visitors in the morning worship service are often looking for a new church home. By and large, the decision may rest on the impression made by the preacher in that one message. No pastor wants to be evaluated on the basis of a single sermon any more than a baseball player wants his batting average to depend upon one inning.

Conflicts with other church members may result in the loss of important relationships. Longtime friends may have a falling-out over some issue. The result can be most devastating. It is not uncommon for members to drop out after the severance of such ties. At times, the entire church may be involved in conflict which, left unchecked, may lead to a split.

"He comes up to me and smiles and shakes my hand. But I wish he'd say, 'I'm sorry.' " Through this confession an inactive member revealed his conflict with another member in the church. That problem stared him straight in the face every time he attend church. The unresolved conflict drained worship of its significance.

It is impossible to know the many interpersonal conflicts with which members may be struggling. Someone outside the membership of the church, such as a family member, may be a source of conflict. An unconverted spouse or parent can exert tremendous pressure on a believer concerning his relationship with the church. A wife was confronted by an abusive husband who threatened to shoot her if she went to church. She replied: "If you kill me, I'm going to heaven. And if you don't, I'm going to church!" Hopefully, such circumstances are rare. Many Christians do face strained relationships with loved-ones and friends over the issue of church.

Theological issues can become a dividing line between members. Often doctrinal disputes are the result of majoring on minor issues. In days of theological diversity and controversy, churches tend to polarize toward a certain theological emphasis. Some churches champion social ministry while others underscore evangelism. The worship style of one church may be characterized by informal, exultant praise. Another church may conduct subdued and reserved services. No two churches are exactly alike. Consequently, a member may feel more comfortable in one kind of church than in another.

Another common generator of conflict is monetary policy. Financial issuess can easily become a source of conflict as money represents power, influence, and values. Those who desire power and authority in the church will naturally seek control of the budget. Differences in priorities among members become graphically obvious in discussions of financial decisions. These tensions become exacerbated when a church is strained to meet its budget.

Not to be forgotten are those who just cannot tolerate conflict. They may fall out of the church fellowship because of conflict which is not even directly related to them. Peace-loving persons can become agitated during times of confrontation. Larry L. McSwain and William Treadwell, Jr. in *Conflict Ministry in the Church,* discussed flight as one of the unhealthy but common ways church members deal with conflict.

> One can simply withdraw from the arena of conflict. Withdrawal happens when people change church memberships in order to keep from becoming involved. Withholding of money for church programs, refusing to vote on either side of an issue, and nonparticipation in church activities are withdrawal actions. Many inactive church members have become so because of conflicts they have fled."[3]

After a particularly argumentative deacons meeting, a deacon commented to me, "I felt like crawling under my chair." So great was the embarrassment over a conflict of which he was not even a participant.

This man developed a sense of dread over future deacons meetings. The fallout resulting from church conflict may be those members who are simply retreating from the tension.

Unmet Expectations

Frustrated expectations of members is the second reason for inactivity. This frustration is very similar to conflict, except that it is more passive. I may have conflict with you because of what you do or say. I will become frustrated by what you do not do or say.

Members' expectations of their pastor are many. He is expected to be dynamic, friendly, above reproach, intelligent, congenial, and so on. A moral failure, a forgotten appointment, or even a missed hospital visit on the part of the pastor can be disappointing to a member. Any pastor can tell you how hard it is to fulfill all the different expectations placed upon him. Harder still is the task of discerning what these expectations may be. One lady was quite upset to see her pastor mowing his lawn without a shirt on. That was not her idea of being above reproach! Obviously, the expectations of members and pastors alike may be unrealistic and doomed to disappointment.

Personal relationships within the church are a crucial aspect of member activity. Members with many friendships within the church are more likely to remain active than those with few friends. Members have social expectations of their church concerning things like socio-economic class, quality of fellowship, and status.

As mentioned before, the style of worship or ministry programs has a bearing on many members' contentment. Persons are likely to become inactive when these things are changed. If someone joined a church because of its classical music, they would obviously be disappointed if the music style were changed to contemporary.

Dedicated and committed members are susceptible to another form of dissatisfaction. As responsibilities are heaped upon these willing servants, there may come a time when they simply become burned out. These members have expectations of themselves and of God which are not being met. What caused them to accept so much work?

Are they zealous for the Lord's work? Do they feel inadequate unless they prove themselves? Is guilt their basic motivation?

One couple in the church had not received Christ as Savior until they were in their thirties. It seemed that they were trying to catch up to the spiritual maturity of their peers. They became overactive in the church. Jim, who owned a struggling business, taught Sunday School and served on several committees. He soon became chairman of the deacons. Fran became a director in the youth division in spite of lingering health problems from a recent illness. A decision to remodel their home gave this couple a break in the pace. Poor attendance was blamed on demands with the house. Before long they dropped out altogether and began visiting another church in their neighborhood. Persons like Jim and Fran need help in relinquishing overbearing responsibilities graciously without a sense of chagrin.

Lack of Affinity

Churches tend to be composed of like-minded people, according to the homogeneous unit principle of church growth. In other words, church members have something in common. They are generally of the same socioeconomic class and geographical area. In addition, a large percentage of members join a specific church because they know someone in that church.

Conversely, when a member senses that he has little in common with other members, he feels uncomfortable. Perhaps a close friend in the church has moved away or died. Churches change over a period of years, as do individuals. New members come in. The faces are different. One may no longer feel at home.

A well-loved Sunday School teacher suddenly passed away. Some of her class members had ridden to church with her each Sunday. Now, with their teacher and friend gone, they lost their desire to attend Sunday School. It just wasn't the same anymore. They had lost their affinity for the church.

Lack of affinity may also be understood as boredom. A member can no longer find any relationship between the church and his own goals and values. This becomes a serious issue. A moral activist grows disheartened with his church's lack of zeal. A single mother finds no commonality with her young married classmates. The disenfranchised youth cannot identify with his elderly minister. An enthusiastic worshiper feels inhibited by the traditional worship of her downtown church. A reticent member feels threatened by the discussion method of his new Sunday School teacher.

Inability to Relate

Some members have a problem being satisfied in whatever church they attend. This particular breed can hold consecutive memberships in a large number of churches in a surprisingly short period of time. They are called "church hoppers." In a category all to themselves, they are unable to get along with practically everyone. Daniel Bagby refers to these inactive members as a special variety whose goal is to remain unrelated and uncommitted, "seeking rejection by virtue of extremely authoritarian postures no congregation would accept."[4]

Members of this category seem to be misfits. The problems they complain about in the church are actually problems they experience within themselves. They take the problems with them wherever they go. As a result they have a problem developing meaningful relationships with others.

Fortunately, there are few of these misfits, but they are unforgettable. One I will always remember was a man who came to our church unhappy about a development in his previous church. Of course, he left our church unhappy as well. Three churches later, he finally found another congregation to join in which he could make his unforgettable impressions.

This chapter has been an overview of the broad reasons why church members drop out. There are psychological and spiritual undercurrents of inactivity which surface in the form of behavior described above. These deeper dimensions of inactivity are covered in chapters two and three.

Application

1. What were the four broad classifications of reasons for inactivity? What is the difference between a reason and an excuse?

2. How did the above discussion make you feel? Could you personally relate to any of the reasons given? What kept you from becoming inactive when you had experiences similar to those just described? How do you feel about the inactive members in your church? Ready to serve? Or, more disillusioned than ever?

3. List inactive members in your church who come to mind when you think of each of the above categories. Write out a brief summary of their story. Be deliberate enough to let forgotten facts come to mind. What are your feelings about each situation (helplessness, anger, hope, guilt, frustration, resentment, grief)?

4. Can you think of other reasons not mentioned? Is there any way you can put these reasons within one of the categories? Can you think of any other categories?

Notes

[1]Jones, Project Report, p. 83.

[2]Lyle E. Schaller, Forward to Leadership and Conflict, by Speed B. Leas (Nashville: Abingdon, 1982), p. 7.

[3]Larry L. McSwain and William C. Treadwell, Jr., Conflict Ministry in the Church (Nashville: Broadman Press, 1981), p. 42.

[4]Daniel G. Bagby, Understanding Anger in the Church (Nashville: Broadman Press, 1979), pp. 27-28.

2
Anxiety
(Psychological Dimensions of Inactivity)

As we have seen, members may withdraw from active participation in the church because they feel uncomfortable about something. This feeling of discomfort is called anxiety.

Centuries of preaching and talking about why members should be active has not really solved the problem of inactivity. Your church can confront inactive members with their "sin" of "forsaking the assembling of yourselves together." You can take them off the church rolls for their inactivity. But until you begin to understand inactivity and reach out to these hurting persons in ministry, you are not going to significantly address this problem.

The Beginning of Inactivity

Bonnie Smith was church clerk for her small suburban congregation. At each business meeting she would faithfully take notes and type up the minutes before the next meeting. It seemed that at each meeting Doug Couch would find some little error in the minutes that needed to be revised. After several meetings, Bonnie became quite agitated about Doug's corrections. When the nominating committee asked Bonnie to serve as clerk for the new church year she declined. Her involvement in the church declined also. No longer did she attend business sessions. Before long she had resigned her Sunday School class. She began spending more time with her husband at their lake lot on Sundays. "There's a little church on the highway we like to attend when we're at the lake," she told a friend.

Most people who drop out of church do so because of a situation that makes them anxious. Up to 90 percent of inactive church members can recall a specific event that lead to their inactivity! By studing the lives of several of these persons, a common and predictable pattern emerges. First, there is the event that produces the anxiety. Secondly, the member seeks to ease his anxiety by expressing his discomfort. Finally, if not responded to, the member begins to drop of out the church. Let's look at this process in more detail.

The Many Shades of Anxiety

John Savage, a pioneer in the study of member inactivity, in his book *The Apathetic and Bored Church Member* identified four types of anxiety which lead persons to drop out of church. The first form of anxiety is *reality anxiety.* Reality anxiety is being upset or anxious over real events. Your Sunday School teacher really did insult you in front of the whole class. Your husband really did threaten divorce if you attend church. These are verifiable and objective situations which can lead to anxiety.

A second form of anxiety is *neurotic.* When a person imagines that someone hates them, they may be plagued with anxiety caused by presuppositions which exist only in their mind. The person feels like the pastor is preaching right at them or everyone in the church dislikes them. In reality, it just wasn't so. It is important to note that even though the causes of neurotic anxiety are imaginary, the anxiety is real. The pain is as real as that caused by real circumstances.

Moral anxiety exists when a person feels guilt. The pastor may not have been preaching at him, but the message was too close for comfort. Imagine how a woman who just had an affair would feel after a poignant sermon on marriage. Obviously, many of the angry responses or discontentment in the church may be the result of unresolved sin.

The realization that we will one day die is another form of anxiety common to us all: *existential anxiety.* This sense of our limits can create an acute feeling of anxiety. Not only are some persons painfully afraid of death, others are afraid of life. What will today bring? How will I live after retirement? Will my health hold up? Will I be victi-

mized by crime? These are all anxious questions which haunt many
people in the daily pursuits of life.

Simplistic answers to the profound questions of human existence
can be a real deterrent to many church members. Many members are
not as worried about making it to heaven as they are about making
it until the next payday. The church should teach us how to live as
well as how to die. Eternal life is an important topic of discussion, but
present concerns may take precedence from time to time.

Expressing the Rage

Members deal with their anxiety in a number of ways. Generally,
people will find a way to express their apprehension. These expressions are the early warning signs that a member is on his way out. If
not responded to, these outcries will fade away into indifference and
inactivity.

One of the common ways of dealing with anxiety is to convert it
into anger. Anger and frustration are first cousins. Studies indicate
that anger responses often arise from thwarted plans or belittling
events.[1] There are innumerable ways members may become frustrated
or feel that they have been looked down upon. Behind those angry
words are the sounds of a wounded spirit or frustrated zeal. As Wayne
Oates observed: "Their anger and resentment are really shrieks of
pain upon having been severely mistreated, neglected, ignored, excluded, and denigrated."[2]

The angry words of a member may be his cry for help. He is really
trying to get the attention of his church so that the situation can be
made right. Different types of personalities will respond to anxiety
and anger in different ways. One person will respond to anxiety in a
direct, outspoken way. Another person will respond in more subtle
ways. Direct persons are likely to be candid, confrontational, and
perhaps lacking in a sense of timing. The direct approach may be
self-defeating by alienating the very ones the angry member is trying
to reach.

The indirect approach of responding to anger will likely employ
subtlety. The subtle person will internalize the anger, seeking to

ignore it. Such an approach may lead to depression. Another indirect approach is the manipulation approach. Anger responses are disguised in the form of spreading rumors and negative comments in a underground form of guerilla warfare. This approach can be extremely destructive to the life of a congregation. It avoids open, direct, and creative dialogue and fosters withdrawal. One-third of inactive members have withdrawn from their church in anger.[3]

Slipping Away

By withdrawing from the church and the source of anxiety, members like Bonnie Smith are cutting themselves off from any possibility of resolving the situation. In fact, withdrawal may serve only to heighten the sense of anxiety. When a member's initial reactions are not noticed or responded to, anxiety increases, creating further withdrawal. Ultimately, this anxiety leads to decreased worship attendance, neglect of committee and other group involvement, and a curtailing of financial support for the church. The member is tacitly telling his church of his unhappiness by pulling away from the fellowship.

The longer these withdrawal actions continue, the less likely it is that the member will be reclaimed. Members may hold out hope of ministry for about six to eight weeks. Then they will begin to set their inactivity in concrete.[4] Any effective ministry of reclamation must occur during this crucial time.

If left unhealed, anger becomes entrenched in a person's life. It is not uncommon for members who have been inactive for a long time to still respond with anger when contacted by the church. A church secretary was verbally assaulted on the telephone by an inactive member who had just received the church's newsletter. Wanting to be removed from the mailing list, this member exhibited a great deal of anger. After being contacted at a later time, this member would not give any reason for becoming inactive. Again the person displayed tremendous anger. Obviously, some form of anxiety had been converted into a dynamo of hostility.

How many of the members of your church have slipped away from the grasping hands of ministry? What can you do to reach through the walls of hostility to reclaim them?

By now you are probably thinking of many committed and very active members of your church who have remained active in spite of having experienced the kinds of anxiety described above. Perhaps you have a hunch that there must be more to it than just anxiety. You're right. Some members seem to persist in service although they may have problems getting along with others in the church. They press on in spite of harsh circumstances in their lives that might keep another member from being active. Something deeper in the lives of these members keeps them going. That is the subject of the next chapter.

Application

1. Briefly describe the process involved in members becoming inactive. What are the various stages of inactivity? Looking back to the study of the inactive members of your church done in the last chapter, at what stage of inactivity are each of these persons? How long has each individual been inactive? Which of these members are in that crucial stage when they are the most receptive to ministry?

2. What are the four types of anxiety presented in this chapter. Can you classify any of the persons in your working list? What was it that made them anxious? What can be done to alleviate that anxiety now?

Notes

[1]A. Anastasia, W. Cohen, and D.A. Spatz, "A Study of Fear and Anger in College Students Through the Controlled Diary Method," *Journal of General Psychology* 73 (1948):243, cited by John S. Savage, *The Apathetic and Bored Church Member* (Pittsford: LEAD Consultants, Inc., 1976), p. 25.

[2]Wayne E. Oates, Forward to *Understanding Anger in the Church,* by Daniel G. Bagby (Nashville: Broadman Press, 1979), p. 5.

[3]Bagby, *Understanding Anger,* pp. 19-27.

[4]Savage, *Apathetic,* pp.

3
The Kingdom of God
(Spiritual Dimensions of Inactivity)

The baffled boys scratched their heads as they watched the automatic door at the new shopping center in their small country town. When a customer approached the door, it would automatically open and then close behind him. Scratching his head in bewilderment, one youngster said to his companion, "How do it know?"

The spiritual issues involved in activity and inactivity are like a complex maze. Often it is hard to know what opens the door of a person's life to the gospel and what closes it. In this chapter, I am going to lead you through this maze of actions, goals, priorities, values, and relationships in the lives of persons. The guidebook for our spiritual journey is the Bible. Get yours handy, you're going to need it. Find the Sermon on the Mount in Matthew 5—7.

What are the parts of the puzzle? Actions, goals, priorites, values, and relationships? What is this potpourri of ethical jargon? These are spiritual issues. How do they relate to inactivity? How do they relate to one another? In our continuing search for the answer to the inactivity question, we are about to enter the heart of the matter.

The Church and the Kingdom

Just a cursory study of the teachings of Jesus shows that our Lord actually spoke very little about the church. In fact, He used the word "church" only twice (Matt. 16:18; 18:17). But, Christ spoke often of the kingdom of God. Many of the parables are illustrations of the kingdom. What is the kingdom? I like to think of the kingdom of God as anywhere Jesus is Lord. Of course, this requires that the kingdom

31

be the domain of the heart. Who or what is running the show in your life? What is it (or who is it) that really determines what your actions will be? That is a kingdom question.

The Sermon on the Mount is really an exposition by our Lord of the principles of the kingdom of God. Why is it that the demands of the Sermon on the Mount are so difficult? Jesus said that not only is murder wrong but so it hatred. Adultery can be committed in one's heart without ever touching another person. The standards of the Sermon on the Mount are so challenging because in the sermon Jesus internalized the law. The kingdom of God is really inside a person. It is one thing to look righteous in your behavior and appearance, but real righteousness come from the heart.

Why is it so hard to live up to the Sermon on the Mount? We live in a world that doesn't operate by the principles laid down by Jesus. People do hate one another and lust after one another. People in our world do not always think of others and their moral responsibilities. You easily surmise that if you live by the Sermon on the Mount, the world will run right over you! You're right, it will! It ran over Jesus!

But, the kingdom of God is the sovereign rule of God. It cannot be defeated and though defeated will ultimately overcome. It is the power of God.

Right in the middle of the Sermon on the Mount, Jesus gave us the Lord's Prayer (Model Prayer) (Matt. 6:9-13). This is the prayer for the subjects of the kingdom: Christians. Jesus taught us to pray, "Thy kingdom come." That is our perspective and prayer. The kingdom of God is a coming kingdom. That it is coming implies a working toward, a development. As Christians, we are still working for the kingdom and it is being worked into our lives. So, an inactive church member is simply someone who is struggling hard with the coming kingdom. The kingdom has yet to be internalized into their lives. But, how do we know that the kingdom is in us?

Who Are We in This World?

Let us look now at three kingdom questions which will help us understand what the kingdom means to our lives. The first question the kingdom asks of us is, Who are we in this world? This is the *relational question*. Who we are has to do with our relationships. If I tell you who I am, I might say that I am my father's son, my daughter's father, my wife's husband, or my church's pastor. I cannot really define who I am without talking about how and with whom I am related.

In the kingdom, our relationships go forth in two directions: vertically (with God) and horizontally (with others). These two planes of relating (vertical and horizontal) are inseperable. Our relationship with God is related to our relationships with others. Jesus made this painfully plain in the Sermon, "For if ye forgive men their trespasses, your heavenly Father will also forgive you: But if ye forgive not men their trespasses, neither will your Father forgive your trespasses" (Matt. 6:14-15). As John says, "If a man say, I love God, and hateth his brother, he is a liar: for he that loveth not his brother whom he hath seen, how can he love God whom he hath not seen?" (1 John 4:20).

Scripturally, the believer is the child of God. This is the vertical dimension. We have been adopted into His spiritual family. This makes us brothers and sisters, which is the horizontal dimension. The believer is said to be "in Christ." He is related to God in Christ. However, the nonbeliever is still separated from God by his sin. Paul refers to the nonbeliever as a "natural man" in 1 Corinthians 2:14: "But the natural man receiveth not the things of the Spirit of God: for they are foolishness unto him; neither can he know them, because they are spiritually discerned."

How a person relates to others is an indication of how established the kingdom of God is in his life. The person who is in Christ relates to God and others differently from the natural man. Let's look at this difference in three ways: the life purpose, kingdom orientation, and relationship status. The *life purpose* describes that for which the person is living. The place of authority in a person's life is referred to as the *kingdom orientation*. The nature of a person's relationships with God and others is termed the *relationship status*.

For the natural man, the life purpose is summed up in Ephesians 2:1-3:

> And you hath he quickened, who were dead in trespasses and sins; Wherein in time past ye walked according to the course of this world, according to the prince of the power of the air, the spirit that now worketh in the children of disobedience: Among whom also we all had our conversation in times past in the lusts of our flesh, fulfilling the desires of the flesh and of the mind; and were by nature the children of wrath, even as others.

This is a person who exalts himself and seeks to build his own kingdom. He seeks to advance his own causes and concerns.

The kingdom orientation of the natural man is egocentric, or self-centered. All of life revolves around him; he is the center of things. Look what this self-centered purpose has done to his relationship status. His relationship with God is broken and his relationships with others are affected. He sees himself as lord and others as subjects in his own little kingdom. He becomes utilitarian as he seeks to use and manipulate others into accomplishing his own goals. This self-centeredness creates conflict. As James explains: "From whence come wars and fightings among you? come they not hence, even of your lusts that war in your members?" (4:1).

This can be seen so clearly in the biblical record of the first family. Eve ate of the forbidden fruit because she saw that it was attractive and would make one wise. She wanted to be like God, knowing good and evil. She had bought into the deception of thinking she could be God Almighty. Adam fell with her and their children also. Their son Abel was murdered by his brother. What was the issue? Worship! Cain's sacrifice was not acceptable to God and his reaction led to Abel's death. The breach in man's relationship with God created a breach in his relationships with his fellowman.

In comparison, the life purpose of the man in Christ is described in Galatians 2:20:

> I am crucified with Christ: nevertheless I live; yet not I, but Christ liveth

in me: and the life which I now live in the flesh I live by the faith of the
Son of God, who loved me, and gave himself for me.

The Christian seeks to exalt Jesus as Lord and is working to build up
God's kingdom. Rather than seek to usurp God's rightful place as
Creator, the Christian is content to fulfill his role as a creature made
in the image of God to bring glory to God. His kingdom orientation
is therefore theocentric, or God-centered (Col. 1:17). Since Christ is
enthroned in his heart and all of life centers around the Savior, the
Christian relates to others on this basis. His relationship status is that
he is reconciled to God through Christ and therefore can be reconciled to others, living in harmonious relationships with other reconciled persons. Instead of trying to get others to fulfill his desires and
purposes, he adopts the servant mindset of the apostle, "I am made
all things to all men, that I might by all means save some" (1 Cor.
9:22).

A fad in bumper stickers uses the symbol of the heart. I have seen
bumper stickers that say, "I [heart] my dog," meaning "I love my
dog." In this way people display their affection for their favorite radio
station, sport, or city. One day, however, I saw a heart bumper sticker
which said, "We [heart] people." It was an advertisement for a
church! How appropriately Christian that was! While the world is
concerned about what they love, the church loves others with the love
of Him who "so loved the world, that he gave his only begotten Son."
What and who we love says a lot about our aims.

What Are We After in This World?

So far we've talked about relationships. Now its time to talk about
values, priorities, and goals. These are all part of the answer to the
discipline question (in ethics its called teleology). What is the discipline question? It has to do with the way we live, it is the ability to
master one's self. A disciplined soldier will keep fighting when the
battle gets hot. Why? To win the war! A disciplined athlete will keep
running when his body is exhausted. Why? To win the race! A higher

purpose is always considered. Temporary discomfort and hardship are worth it in order to attain something important.

Every person is driven by some high (though not necessarily noble) purpose. It is their life's dream, their purpose in life. For some it is to get rich; for others, to learn. For some, the dream seems too impossible and they give up. Whatever form it may take, it represents the values, priorities, and goals of a person's life—the driving force.

What are values? Values represent what is important to us. People place value on money, other people, and power. Priorities are simply those things upon which we place the highest value. If we can't have everything we want, then we will strive for what is most important to us.

Goals are where the wheels of value and the rubber of priority hit the road. Goals are plans, whether written out and carefully strategized or just an ambition in the back of our minds. Goals are values and priorities put into intentions—when you actually plan to do something.

Goals arise from our priorities. We attempt to achieve or attain those things most important to us. Where did the priorities come from? Our values. And where did our values come from? Our relationships!

In church we talk much about our relationship to God. We say we love God and one another. That is all good. But, our relationship to God will determine what our values, priorities, and goals are. It is inescapable! If attending church, worshiping, reading the Bible, praying, witnessing, and ministering are important to us, it is because of our relationship with the Lord.

You don't just decide that something is important to you, it either is or isn't, automatically. You may say something is important, but that's no guarantee that it is. Every day in this country men and women tell each other at the altar of marriage that they love, honor, and cherish one another and that they will remain faithful always. Yet, the divorce rate is soaring. Where does it break down? In the relationships!

In this sense, there is not much difference between divorced persons and inactive members. Both have made a grand profession and a public commitment. Both have renigged. It's gone sour. Perhaps they've been cheating or cheated; abusive or abused. They've lost interest. Its just not worth it anymore. If the relationship had been right, there would have been no departure!

Then there is the guilt. Guilt is when what should be does not equal what is. This results in anxious feelings. A member may experience such feelings when he is in the presence of someone who represents the standards of his morality, which he is not living up to. One young person was immediately plunged into guilt anxiety when he answered the doorbell while high on drugs. On the porch was his pastor!

In churches we spend a lot of time talking about and working on values, priorities, and goals. We try to get people to come more, give more, do more, love more, share more, pray more, study more, and even sing more. Maybe we should spend more words and time on relationships! There is no such thing as a nonrelational gospel! If the relationships were right, then the behavior would follow. The most important thing in the church is not how much money we bring in, or how many people we bring in, or how big our buildings are, but how we are related to one another in Christ.

What Did We Do in This World?

The room is dim. The ceiling is crisscrossed by the rails of the white, hung ceiling panels. Where are you? You've just awakened in a strange place. Strange sounds. Strange smells. Strange feelings. It was your own pain that awakened you. Strong pain. A dull throbbing in your chest and an echoing beep. You are in an intensive care unit. The words are arrested in your throat by a hose. You say to yourself, "Now I understand what that guy was talking about in that book I was reading on inactive members—existential anxiety—I think I'm dying!" You are.

As you mentally die in this imaginary illustration, slowing passing away on your death bed, think of your real life. Your childhood, the storms of adolesence, your family, your career, the catastrophy that brought you where you are today. Its almost over. What will you leave behind? What were you able to accomplish in your lifetime?

You've just been introduced to the third kingdom question, the *fruit question*. In the Sermon on the Mount, Jesus said:

> "Therefore take no thought, saying, What shall we eat? or, What shall we drink? or, Wherewithal shall we be clothed? (For after all these things do the Gentiles seek:) for your heavenly Father knoweth that ye have need of all these things. But seek ye first the kingdom of God, and his righteousness; and all these things shall be added unto you" (Matt. 6:31-33).

There is something to positive thinking. I believe that what you seek with your whole heart is pretty much what you will get in life. The question is, What are you seeking? When you look back over your life and see all the things you have gotten and accomplished, how will you feel about it? Was it really what you wanted?

I once noticed a newspaper article about a California computer executive who died in a car wreck just hours after becoming a millionaire. A lifelong dream achieved—on the last day of life? If God allowed you but one dream to see come true, what would it be?

What inactive members are telling us by their lack of activity in the church is that their dreams are different from ours. Perhaps their dream looked impossible so they opted out for a more practical fulfillment—a lesser dream. Can you help them recapture the vision? To dream the dream again?

The twelve disciples were men with a dream. They looked for the hope of Israel. One day their Dream died. They were "scattered as sheep without a shepherd," as men without a dream. But, the resurrected Lord lovingly and gently restored the dream. The dream lives on! Their love for Jesus shook the world!

That is what the ministry of reclamation is: helping those who love Jesus to dream again.

Application

1. What is the difference between the kingdom of God and the church?

2. What are the three kingdom questions presented in this chapter?

3. How is relationship with Christ and other believers related to a person's activity in a local church? As you look over the list of inactive members of your church, are any such relationship problems apparent to you in the lives of these persons?

4. What is the basis for our values, priorities, and goals? What does lack of participation in the church tell you about a member's values, priorities, and goals?

5. Is there a connection between a person's dreams and accomplishments in life? How can you help the inactive members of your church to once again find importance in being active in their church? List some actions you can take. Analyze the appropriateness of the following actions meant to reclaim inactive members:

- A strongly worded sermon about the evils of backsliding.
- An invitation to a church social.
- A letter from the deacons warning of removal from membership.
- A call from a Sunday School teacher inviting them to attend class.
- A loving visit from the pastor and/or a deacon.
- An evangelistic visit.
- A conversation with a loved one or friend of the member.

4
Is There Enough Room?
(Sociological Dimensions of Inactivity)

Remember Paster Jones back at Faith Church? When we last talked with Jones, he was scratching his head in bewilderment at the growing inactive member statistics of his pastorate. Faith Church is a relatively new congregation and has experienced a steady growth throughout its history, until last year when the growth began to plateau. That was also the same year Jones was called as pastor. Why the stagnation in growth? Why the increasingly large numbers of inactive members?

To fully examine any church situation and discover the reasons for halted growth and inactivity is a very complex matter! Thus far we have examined the psychological and spiritual reasons for inactivity. But there may be some other factors involved—factors so simple and obvious that they defy recognition. These are sociological factors. It would be extremely difficult to see these factors by examining reasons for the inactivity of a specific individual member. But, let us take an overall look at the church and see these forces that are silently and inconspicuously at work in every church.

A sociological factor is distinct from the mere psychological or spiritual side of persons; it has to do with the way persons relate to one another in groups. Since a church is a group (and often a group of groups), sociological factors play a major role in the health of the church. This may not sound very "spiritual," but I think you'll agree that it is realistic and practical.

If Faith Church is a typical church, it has reached a hurdle. The church has grown in membership and attendance. Every one of its birthdays celebrated an increase in numbers—until recently. What is wrong with Faith Church? Is it the pastor? The deacons or board? Is it the neighborhood?

Before Jones can really address the inhibitors to his church's progress and the reasons why so many of his parishioners are inactive, he will have to look at the problem from every angle. One very crucial angle from which to view inactivity is the sociological angle. In this chapter we will examine five sociological factors that are inherent in the health of a congregation.

Providing Enough Space

A common challenge for college students is to see how many of them can get into a Volkswagen or telephone booth. Most Volkswagens are designed to comfortably (that may be stretching it!) seat four people. Telephone booths are built to accommodate one person at a time. However, the law of Sophomore Silliness states that on occasion as many as a dozen students may be crammed into a Volkswagen and perhaps half that many into a telephone booth. I was never asked to participate in such folly because I displace the mass of two average humans!

Your church may be suffering from the Volkswagen complex. You have reached the comfortable capacity of your facilities. The purpose of this book is not to give you square footage formulas for building space. There are plenty of expert sources for this information. But, this might be an issue in your church.

Your church may be like the television commercial that showed a marching band marching into a Volkswagen! The TV camera was placed so that you could not see the marchers crawling out the other side as each person jumped in! This is what happens in churches on occasion. Because of the limitations of space, every time someone joins the church and begins attending regularly someone else quits attending regularly! You may still have new members coming in the front door, but you also have a flow of members leaving out the back door. Most of these members may be joining another church, but some are simply becoming inactive.

Without giving you a lot of formulas and figures, there are some rules of thumb that come in handy. Sanctuary space: you are full when you reach 80 per cent of the comfortable seating capacity. Don't forget to include the choir loft. Sociologically speaking, people are not sardines! Most people feel too cramped in a room at maximum capacity. They may tolerate it for sixty seconds on an elevator, but they won't tolerate it for sixty minutes in a sanctuary! Your sanctuary can be too big, too. The crowd looks too small if the room is not filled to at least 50 percent seating capacity.

Of course there are exceptions to all of these rules. But, the inactive members of your church are probably not the exceptions!

Parking lots: you need approximately one space for every three persons in attendance. Also, there should be some empty spaces in the lot at the peak attendance times. The quality of the lot and accessibility are also factors. The parking lot should be as nice as your church can make it, preferably cement or asphalt with a professional striping job. However, it should be at least as nice as what the members are accustomed to at home and work. In some situations, you can get by with gravel.

Classrooms: children need more room than adults. Too often the children are assigned the poorest facilities. If you want to reach and keep families, give your best to the children. This goes for workers, too!

Let me say a word about bus ministries. But ministries tend to be exclusively children oriented. There is nothing wrong with this. But, be aware that this type of ministry will make super demands upon your church to provide space, workers, and finances. A well-staffed, properly administered, and adequately funded bus ministry can be a tremendous outreach tool and ministry. Conversely, a bus ministry maintained by a minimum amount of workers, administration, and money can serve as a black hole of energy, sucking the life out of workers and the program of the church. If not done properly, a bus ministry can leave you with a host of worn-out, frustrated, and inactive members!

Providing Enough Services

The conflict and unmet expectations of inactive members may result from frustrations over a lack of services. Do not misunderstand, *no church can meet all the needs of every person.* There is a minimum bottom line for services, however, for every church. Each church has its own capabilities, resources, and opportunities. Each church should do the best it can with what it has. The question to ask at this point is, "Are we, as a church body, adequately ministering to the needs of our members?"

I'm sorry, but I know of no rules of thumb for services. It would be safe to say that, in general, the larger the church, the more services it can provide. Also, variety comes with size. But, be not dismayed! Most churches are small churches! Your small church cannot compete with the large regional churches in providing a variety of quality services, but you can find a need and meet it. Small churches may have to specialize to survive.

I know of a church that is composed largely of senior adults. At first, one might think this little church has little to offer. To the contrary! They are a healthy, dynamic congregation. The staff is composed of senior adults and the ministry of the church centers around seniors. It is an exciting church and has found its niche in ministry. This church could not possibly provide adequate services for the youth or young adults in the community, but it can provide a wide range of quality services for senior adults.

Fast and sensational growth can be achieved in a number of ways: advertisement, entertainment, or hype. But lasting growth numerically and spiritually is the result of ministry to the needs of persons. One important rationale and impetus for church programs should be the felt needs of the members of your congregation.

Providing Enough Fellowship

Biblically, fellowship *(koinonia)* is the shared life of believers in faith and ministry. These relationships are precious and necessary for healthy Christians and churches. A central hope of my faith is the time I will join with all the redeemed of the ages around the throne of Jesus in heaven! Heaven is going to be great, and one of the reasons for its greatness is fellowship—fellowship with Christ and with the millions of saints!

Sometimes we get so caught up in the heavenly vision that we lose sight of an important sociological principle. In heaven we will fellowship with the hosts of the redeemed, but on earth we can only have a significant fellowship with thirty-five to eighty persons at any one time!

How many friends do you have whom you know by name and comfortably associate with on a regular basis? If you are typical, that number will be somewhere in the range mentioned above. "Well," you ask, "if that's true, how is that we have much more than that in our worship services every Sunday?" Because you do not have to know people personally and by name to worship together!

Most Christians want to associate with a group of Christians. This association can be meaningful as fellowship if the group is between thirty-five to eighty in size. If the group gets larger than this, members start losing touch with one another. Some will complain that the group is getting too big. They cannot possibly learn everyone's name and get to know them personally.

If your church is much larger than eighty in active membership, you will have more than one of these fellowship groups within the congregation. Virtually every active member is a part of one or more of these groups. The groups may be the choir, Bible study group, or some ministry group.

A church can get to the point that these groups are at their maximum capacity. There is no room left in the fellowship groups for more persons to be involved. So, what happens? As new persons come into the church and are incorporated into one of these bloated groups, somebody drops out. Perhaps the "doors" to the groups are closed and the new members cannot find inclusion. At that point, the new members drop out. These members may join another church where they can be included in a fellowship group, or they may just remain inactive and find provision for their social needs in a secular group.

Providing Enough Intimacy

Second Avenue Church averages about sixty in attendance. This small community church is thirty-five years old. The community has changed a great deal in those years, and the church has long since seen its best years numerically. Jim Spencer, a new resident to the old community, has recently joined Second Avenue. He was a regular fixture at morning worship for several weeks. Gradually Jim seemed to lose interest and now comes once every month or so. What happened?

To understand the problem of Second Avenue, let's take the idea of the fellowship group a step further. Second Avenue Church is small enough to be a fellowship group in itself, and this is pretty much the case. Even though this fellowship group has not yet reached its maximum capacity Jim is having trouble finding inclusion. By now Jim knows most of the active attenders by name and is greeted warmly each time he attends. Jim enjoys the fellowship of Second Avenue.

In terms of a fellowship, Second Avenue has room to grow, even as a single-fellowship church. But, Second Avenue has intimacy problems. Jim has not yet been accepted into the deeper level of fellowship. To most of the members, Jim is a newcomer. They do not intentionally exclude him from close relationships; it is just that most of the members have known each other for decades. They have been a part of the church for over twenty years. How can Jim possibly understand and appreciate the long-term closeness of these older members?

The old building of Second Avenue Church is spacious. Only a fraction of the parking lot is used. The membership is small. But, Second Avenue has no vacancies for intimacy.

Intimacy takes place in the context of small groups. These groups are between eight and twelve persons. It is in these small groups that the deep and meaningful experiences of Christian living are shared.

At times, Jesus had thousands of disciples who followed Him. But, He chose only twelve to be apostles. It was into the lives of this small group of men that Jesus poured His life. He shared with them the lessons of the kingdom of God and led them personally.

It may be that many of the inactive members of your church were simply not able to find entry into a small group within the congregation. They could not find those few persons who would befriend them and share with them the mutual experiences of life.

Is your church saturated at the point of intimacy? To illustrate, take a glass of warm water. Mix into the water a teaspoon of salt. As the salt soon dissolves, the water becomes clear again. Now, mix in another teaspoon, and another, and another. Before long it will become harder and harder to dissolve the salt into the water. Soon, salt deposits will form at the bottom of the glass as the solution of salt and water becomes saturated. Water can only absorb so much salt. In the same way your church can only absorb so many members in the groups now present.

In order to provide more intimacy, more small groups must be formed. Bible study groups, prayer groups, committees, and ministry groups all provide more opportunities for members to be included. Furthermore, the avenues for entrance into these small groups must be wide open or members will drop out for lack of intimacy.

Providing Enough Leadership

Another thing Jim Spencer noticed about the workings of Second Avenue Church was the way decisions were made. Jim always attended the business sessions. At first he would even voice his opinions about certain issues. Soon Jim began to feel that the decisions had already been made before the meeting was held and before the vote was taken. There was obviously an inner circle of influence within the church. Furthermore, it was a closed circle.

In terms of leadership, most churches are like a pyramid. A relatively small number of members hold the greatest amount of influence. This is true regardless of the official polity of the church. Is there enough room at the top of the pyramid in your church for new blood?

Many members are content to allow the involved, articulate, and competent members of the congregation to dominate the decision-making process. They are followers. So long as things are going well at the church, they see no problem with this. They will just go along.

But, it is discouraging for an enthusiastic and committed member to constantly be denied input into the real decision-making process. He will conclude that he is not wanted and will drop out. Why beat one's head again the brick wall of the informal and established hierarchy?

As you get to know the inactive members of your church and seek to discern their particular reasons for inactivity, you may find these reasons are rooted in sociological factors. The task that confronts you will then become much more involved than just the reclaiming of an inactive member; it may be the reclaiming of the church!

Application

1. What is the difference between a psychological cause of inactivity and a sociological factor?

2. What were the five sociological factors presented in this chapter?

3. Using the rules of thumb given, evaluate the facilities of your church. What specific actions can be taken to alleviate any problems you discover?

4. Are the services provided by your church adequate to meet the needs of your members? Utilizing the insights given, what steps can your church take toward improving the variety and quality of services? What areas of service should your church focus on?

5. What are some ways the quality of fellowship and intimacy can be improved in your church?

6. In evaluating the decision-making process of your congregation, how can it be more inclusive of the input and involvement of newer members?

II
Theological Foundations

Up to this point we have examined the process of member inactivity from the psychological, spiritual, and sociological perspectives. In this section, we shall examine the spiritual issues more deeply as we probe the theological bases for activity. Any ministry to inactive members must be strongly undergirded with a biblical base. The minister of reclamation must be well versed in the biblical meaning of and rationale for active participation in the local church.

A ministry to inactive members will provide an opportunity for renewal in the church. As the church studies the reasons for its existence and the discipleship of its members, a revival of worship and service is bound to ensue. As the church launches out into a vital ministry to reclaim its dormant members, a revival of fellowship will result. As the church rediscovers the meaning of discipleship and seeks to equip its members to actively share in the ministry of the gospel, a revival of proclamation and teaching will occur.

Reclamation is another word for church discipline. Discipline is a rare part of most churches today, perhaps because of erroneous approaches in the past and a lingering fear of enforcing true discipleship. Rather than viewing discipline as a holy battle of purging the church of dead wood and carnal, backslidden members, discipline should be seen as part of the caring concern of the church, actively seeks the welfare of its own.

If the Christian life is worth living and if the local church is worthy of our participation, then the ministry of reclamation is essential. I approach this subject with a deep burden for the biblical urgency of the task. How can we, the church, seek the lost of this world with integrity if we do not seek the straying believer as well? Have we been lulled into a sense of apathy about the spiritual well-being of our members by a misapplication of such doctrines as the security of the believer and the perseverance of the saints? My prayer is that Christians will come to view reclamation as a central and crucial aspect of church life.

In this section, the theological foundations for activity and reclamation will be presented around two questions. First, what is the theological message inactive members are sending to us by their unwillingness to be active in their church? This is essentially a way of looking at the behavior of drop outs from a biblical perspective. Second, what can and should the church do to reclaim its straying members? This is a question about the responsibility and behavior of the church in reclamation.

5
What Are They Telling Us?

Two deep sea divers were working on a sunken wreck. Suddenly one of the divers began gesturing wildly to the other. "Is it a shark?" the second diver wondered as he signaled his bewilderment. His diving buddy waved his hands wildly. "What is it? The bends?" The panicky diver shook his head no. Then the stricken diver grabbed his underwater writing tablet and grease pencil. Furiously he scribbled a message before passing out.

On board ship, the diver remained puzzled as to what malady had befallen his friend who lay recovering in the sick bay. Looking at the tablet, he finally deciphered the message: 'You-re st-and-ing on my a-ir ho-se!"

How ludicrous this story sounds, yet it illustrates the plight of the concerned churchman who seeks to reclaim his fellow members. One arrives at a point of almost desperately asking what is the matter with the inactive member. Well-meaning concern and attention are focused on the drop-outs in a loving attempt at ministry. These advances are then met by strange responses. To the reclaimer the responses are strange indeed, but to the hurting member, the problem is obvious.

The Pain of Sin's Effect

In this chapter we shall explore the theological and biblical themes involved in inactivity and reclamation. The message most inactive members are wanting, if only unconsciously, to get across to the church is this: "I'm hurting!" So intense is the pain in their hearts that they can become quite emphatic in their expressions of unhappiness.

51

Woe be to the naive do-gooder who is able to unstop the cork of their malcontent!

Let us examine the profound truths of Scripture which shed great light on the problem of inactive members. We must begin in the beginning—creation. God's purpose in creation involves meaningful and fulfilling relationships for man. Man was created, according to the old catechism, "to love God and enjoy Him forever." Man was made in the image of God as a being with which God could have fellowship. In order for this fellowship to be truly meaningful and fulfilling for all concerned, it was necessary that the engineering of human nature include the component of free will. Man was thus made with volitional power to choose. It was a somewhat precarious situation, but God was willing to take the risk, knowing all the while the price He would have to pay for His creative expression of love.

God's relationship with man was that of closeness and intimacy. God walked and talked with man. Out of response to the social needs of man, God created the woman to share in the God-like image. The relational picture of the creation account is breathtakingly beautiful!

But, soon the divine vision of creation was shattered by human sin. Suddenly there was a breech in the fresh intimacy between deity and humanity. Adam and Eve became conscious of their nakedness and hid themselves from God.

The destructive effect of sin upon relationships becomes painfully obvious as one reads the biblical account. In one fatal stroke of its malicious sword, sin severed the ties between God and his human companions and even between humans themselves. Adam and Eve no longer experienced the glorious closeness that before had characterized their relationship. They felt naked before one another, uncomfortable with authentic and transparent openness. More so did they sense a dread of the Lord. Hiding themselves in the jungle of futility, they fled from the holy face of the Lord.

One can almost hear the grieving voice of God as He calls out, "Adam, were are you?" To this day, God seeks His fallen creatures. Lost persons in a fallen world grope for hope and fulfillment. Life loses its meaning for many who see no purpose in the senseless misery of their worlds. Still God is active in His saving pursuit of mankind.

The brokenness of human relationships is graphically portrayed in the continuing record of Genesis. Murder plagued the first family as Cain slew his brother Abel. What was the issue that incited such wrath? Worship. The picture of the degeneration of mankind's relationship with God is complete in the murder of Abel over the acceptability of his sacrifice. Man's enmity against God is lived out against his fellowman. "Am I my brother's keeper?" is the morose question of secular man.

What we are seeing here is the outworking of anxiety. Though we have already discussed anxiety as a pervasive psychological aspect of inactivity, there are some theological considerations about anxiety which need to be explored.

Anxiety has its origin in sin. The first biblical reference to anxiety, or fear, is in the context of the first sin. "I was afraid, because I was naked; and I hid myself," cried the first man in Genesis 3:10. Moses, gripped by awe and fear in the burning bush experience, was told to take his sandals off, for he was standing on holy ground (Ex. 3). Isaiah lamented, "woe is me," in the presence of the holy God, for he had become keenly aware of his sinfulness (Isa. 6). In the presence of the glorified Savior, John fainted (Rev. 1:17). Sin has built a brick wall of anxiety and fear between man and God and between men, as Paul Schmidt says in his book, *Coping with Difficult People.*

> When I speak about character disorders, I am talking about persons who most of all need the help of concerned family and friends in the larger family of the church. These characters have carefully built and guarded some well-fortified walls, and they hide behind these walls from God, from their fellow human beings, and even from themselves. Seen psychologically, they are chiefly unable to give and receive genuine love. Spiritually, they are not living by Jesus' two great commandments to love God above all, and to love others as themselves.[1]

Inactive members are persons who once were active members in a local church. This obvious fact needs to be emphasized. These are people who once made their profession of faith in Christ, claiming His salvation and benefits, committing themselves to His lordship. Yet now they are living out the shattered vision of creation in that their lives are characterized by broken relationships. Though they may remember the sweetness of their conversion and initial entrance into the church, they have yet to experience the full reality of the gospel of peace. They are experiencing a profound brokenness in their relationships with other believers as a blatant contradiction of the gospel promise. The pain of sin's effects has driven them away from the church even though their religious hopes are tied so strongly to the community of fellow believers.

The estrangement from others is a reminder to inactive members of the darkness of their lives before conversion and casts a pallor over their Christian experience. In their inactivity they are acting out this estrangement. Inactivity may even be their way of coping with the pain of these broken relationships. It is often easier and less painful to avoid problems than it is to face them and deal with them constructively.

John and Samantha Jackson were growing more and more frustrated with the financial squeeze their church was experiencing. Much like their own personal financial problems, the church was having trouble paying the bills. John felt he must take the lead and suggest that half of the moneys used for the church's youth program be diverted temporarily toward paying off the bills. The congregation defeated the motion John made. Only one other person sided with the Jacksons in the vote. It was embarrassing! Although the other members were more than cordial to the Jacksons after the meeting, the tension was still there. In spite of visits by the pastor and contacts from other church members, within three months the Jackson family had decided to begin attending another church with some friends. A year later the membership of the inactive family has yet to be moved and contact with them has been nil.

Could the pain of the Jacksons' embarrassment have been a contributing factor in their inactivity? Did they lose a sense of unity with the church? Did they feel alienated and rebuffed? How could they have been reclaimed?

A Denial of Discipleship

Another theological dimension of the pain experienced by inactive members has to do with their view of themselves as followers of Jesus. Biblically, inactivity is indicative of a spiritual condition inconsistent with the Christian profession and mission. The biblical meaning of the believer's profession of faith is the theological foundation of active service and participation within the framework of the church.

The Lordship of Christ

The profession of faith in Christ is in essence a commitment to His lordship as well as a claiming of salvation truths. As DeVern Fromke has said,

> Believers may not often realize it, but even as believers we are either centered on man, or centered on God. There is no alternative. Either God is the center of our universe and we have become rightly adjusted to Him, or we have made ourselves the center and are attempting to make all else orbit around us and for us.[2]

Jesus' words in Luke 14:26-33 to the multitudes following Him, form an example of His demand to be the center of His believers' lives. In summary, Jesus taught in this passage that to profess to be His disciple is tantamount to making the commitment to follow Him as Lord. The cost of discipleship is an all-encompassing surrender. This claim is echoed in Paul's statement in Romans 10:9 that if you "confess with your mouth the Lord Jesus," which states the Christian profession as a surrender to the lordship of Christ. Inactivity belies such a profession. It is this inconsistency, which is stated in the contradiction of terms *inactive* and *member* (part of the body of Christ, citizen of the covenant community), which weighs upon the inactive member's conscience.

Reconciliation

Another theological inconsistency inherent in inactivity is that those members professing to be Christians who are reconciled to God in Christ are in need of reconciliation with their spiritual brethren. Jesus emphasized the imperative of loving one another. "By this," Jesus says, "all men will know that you are my disciples, if you have love for one another" (John 13:35, RSV). His prayer was "that they may all be one; even as thou, Father, art in me, and I in thee, that they also may be in us, so that the world may believe that thou hast sent me" (John 17:21, RSV). As Raymond Ortland expresses it:

> Love is the chief mark of the believer's authenticity. Christ commanded believers to love each other. And what He demands of Christians He also supplies to them. "God has poured out his love into our hearts by the Holy Spirit, whom he has given us" (Rom. 5:5). The fruit of the Spirit includes love (Gal. 5:22). The relationship between believers is secured for them by the Lord Himself as He places His holy deposit of love in their lives. The Holy Spirit, who is the source of love, will supply all the love a Christian needs for all the pepole he will ever meet in all the situations he will ever face. The supply of the Spirit will not fail, even in difficult times.[3]

The reconciliation of the believer to God is tied to the mission for believers to function as witnesses of God's reconciling act in Christ. How valid could such a witness be by those who are yet to be reconciled to their fellow witnesses?

Paul stresses this theme of reconciliation in Romans 8 where he says "There is therefore now no condemnation to them which are in Christ Jesus" (v. 1) as setting forth our reconciliation with God in Christ. This reconciliation involves the Christian's relationship with others since we all, in Christ, are "children of God: and if children, then heirs; heirs of God, and joint-heirs with Christ" (v. 16-17). Are we not then to assume that if we are "joint-heirs with Christ" we are also joint-heirs with one another as God's adopted children (v. 15)?

In writing to the divisive Corinthian Christians (2 Cor. 5), Paul reaffirms the reconciliation of God in Christ with an exhortation that this reconciliation has made of the believer "a new creation" and that all things are of God, who hath reconciled us to himself by Jesus Christ, and hath given to us the ministry of reconciliation" (v. 18). The moral demand of such a calling as ministers of reconciliation is that believers be reconciled to one another. Here again, the link is made between the salvation truth of reconciliation to God in Christ and the commission of believers as reconciliation agents.

Furthermore, the essence of church membership embodies the reality of reconciliation. Persons are made members of the church upon the public profession of their faith in Christ and their obedient baptism.[4] One aspect of the Christian's mission and work is to "work out and exemplify life implanted in regeneration."[5] Inactive members are essentially failing to fulfill their mission in Christ.

This failure precipitates a lack of assurance on the part of many inactive members. It has been my personal experience in talking to inactive members that many of them relate little or no assurance that they indeed are going to heaven when they die, even though they can remember clearly their conversion experience. The great inconsistency between their past professions and present inactivity convinces them that something is dreadfully wrong with their relationship with God.

A member of the church who had slowly become less and less active over a period of months was experiencing a spiritual crisis. In the hospital recovering from an accident, Sally has recurring dreams of dying and being doomed. In her nightmare, she acted the part of a beligerent sinner. She was devastated.How could she say such a thing? Guilt flooded in as she faced with terror the prospects of her own eternal damnation. It was a fate worse than death.

Upon hearing of the woman's grief that morning I went to the hospital for a pastoral visit. Sally was in the bed like a wartime refugee, gathering a blanket around her with one hand and holding a tear-soaked tissue in the other. Upon my entry into the room and initial greetings, the worried family left us alone. She related to me her dream and concluded in a burst of sobs.

During the conversation, a nurse came in to give her a shot for her painful back injury. "Were you having the nightmares before you came to the hospital?" I asked. She shook her head, "No." I then encouraged her to call the doctor before taking any more of the shots and ask him if they could be causing these side-effects, as they sometimes do. She appeared relieved to hear that her midnight renunciation of her Christian faith may have been the result of a narcotic stupor! It was at this point in the conversation that Sally confessed, "You know, Brother Mark, I feel so guilty sometimes that I don't go to church like I should."

Do not underestimate the feelings of guilt the inactive members of your church may be experiencing! The blatant and obvious nature of their spiritual failures sends an undeniable message to them. The message may sound something like, "If you are really a Christian, then why aren't you acting like one?!"

The Quest for Experiential Christianity

While the inactivity of some members evidences their lack of commitment to Christ and signals some very profound problems in their relationship with Him, for others, inactivity is the response of a heart longing for more. It was not their lack of interest in the things of God that led to inactivity, but rather their deep desires for a more meaningful and fulfilling religious experience. The longings of their hearts were not being met in the local church, either because of their inordinate needs or a spiritually shallow church ministry and fellowship.

As Donald and Francine Friedman became increasingly involved in the home fellowship group that met on Thursday nights, their satisfaction with things at Main Street Church proportionately dwindled. The weekday home group was exciting. Each week, members shared the mighty experiences they were having with the Lord. Prayers were being answered right and left. One member's mother was healed of bone cancer. Another couple's marriage was saved. Once, when a group member lost his job, the group took personal responsibility to care for the family until a new job was found. "This is what Christianity is all about," Fran told Don on the way home from a group meeting one night.

In comparison, the Friedman's barely knew the members of their Sunday School class. The worship services at Main Street Church were not nearly as meaningful to them as the singing and prayer time in their group. Besides, with such busy schedules it was becoming hard to find time for church and the fellowship group. Wednesday evening services had already found a substitute in the Thursday evening Bible study. Last Sunday evening Don and Fran went with two other couples in the group to a halfway house to witness to some of the residents. That was much more exhilarating than the missions presentation held at Main Street Church! "I'm tired of talking church. I feel like this is doing church!" Don explained.

Jan Green found Main Street Church uninviting for another reason. "I just don't feel like most of those people would understand," she said to one of the associate pastors right after her hospital stay. Six months ago, Jan was admitted to Lake County Hospital diagnosed with a rare form of leukemia. She was told then by her physician that she had maybe three months to live. Six months later, the disease has remitted and she feels as healthy as ever. Her baffled doctor had simply concluded, "the Lord has smiled on you." She queried her minister, "Why doesn't the church teach healing? It happened to me! I think there's a whole world of power and truth that the church is oblivious to."

The underlying question behind both of these pilgrimage stories is whether or not a reconciling God is active in the lives of persons to lead them to wholeness. Otherwise, the Christian faith is merely the upholding of ancient rules in a mechanistic life of meaninglessness. These inactive members are looking for a life of purposeful religious experience.

But, if one is to live out the vision of reconciliation in experiential Christianity, he must understand something of the nature of experience itself. Is experience that which happens in the life of the believer or the believer's interpretation of what happens in his life? Experience is interrelated to consciousness. Basically, the meaning persons assign to life is tied to their interpretations of reality as experienced.[6]

Experience becomes a vital issue in the ministry of reclamation since some inactivity is related to a need for deeper levels of experience in daily Christian living and a frustration of this need, or desire. In seeking to minister to inactive members, it is important to understand the inner world of the members. What is their experience? What is the meaning of their lives?

Paul Tillich, as he looked for answers to the perplexing dilemmas in life which seem to contradict the vision of God's ultimate good, was concerned that the Christian message about the meaning of life not be misinterpreted in terms of God's providence:

> And such misunderstanding necessarily leads to a disillusionment which not only turns the hearts of men away from God, but also creates a revolt against Him, against Christianity, and against religion . . . Faith in divine Providence is the faith that nothing can prevent us from fulfilling the ultimate meaning of our existence. Providence does not mean a divine planning by which everything is predetermined, as is an efficient machine. Rather, Providence means that there is a creative and saving possibility implied in every situation, which cannot be destroyed by any event."[7]

Some inactive members are struggling with the deep meaning of their lives. This struggle is taking them away from the church due to the conflict in their faith and the realities of life. For them it is a time of reevaluating their beliefs, which is often a painful process. As John Biersdorf points out in his study of vital religious communities, some persons who are deeply involved in such communities had "graduated" from their local churches. Their "hunger for experience," as the title of his work states, had driven them beyond the status quo of a Christian interpretation of life lacking in meaning for them.[8]

A Christianity that overemphasizes the one experience of salvation to the neglect of an understanding of the ongoing journey of daily Christian experience may be largely responsible for the frustrations many believers experience. A renewed emphasis on experience is offered by theologians who

> while affirming the value of decisive spiritual moments and wishing for more genuinely transforming religious experiences, view conversion in a

different way. Conversion is seen as a process in which the discerning believer recognizes that the definitive moment is part of an unfolding pattern in which there has been a series of events and experiences which have moved the person toward the spiritual awakening which has occurred. Furthermore, the conversion moment is seen not as an "arrival" but a "beginning" in which the spiritually awakened person is now empowered to start actualizing the potential which has been inherent in his or her life.[9]

The believer's conception of God-at-work in his daily life is a large determinant of his attitudes towards the church. Those who are hurting in the crucible of disillusionment may be driven away from a religious community which offers pat answers for unfathomable mysteries.

For some, this desire for experiential Christianity leads to inordinate searchings into the territory of the unreal. Consequently, it becomes an ironic struggle: the search for the "real" power of God leading to a fantasy faith. It is interesting to note how often such struggles surface at crisis times, when the believer's faith is shaken and there is an acute sense of need and ambivalence. A great deal of ministry must then be helping persons to develop more of an experiential faith (where belief becomes action) in dealing with the realities of life and God.

In dealing with people's search for the real God in real life, those who minister must be careful not to be cruel in taking away experiences that are meaningful, though the experiences may be very difficult (initially, at least) to understand. There will be opportunities for greater insight at a later time.

A grieving member was almost overcome with the reality of his son's death. He could not cope with life without his little boy. Suddenly he had been taken from him, and now he wept day and night for relief from his misery. Then one afternoon, he walked into my office a new man. The spark had returned to his eyes and the energy to his steps. "Did you hear about my boy?" he said as he met me at the door. Just the day before he had been "visited" by his dead son!

He explained how he appeared in his home and talked with him for about fifteen minutes. He assured him that everything was well and that he was in heaven. I was not about to try to take that experience away from him as much I as disbelieved. It had literally saved his life! Whatever his experience had been, even if just the subconscious invention of his imagination, it was a turning point in his grieving process that enabled him to once again face the present and future.

As Victor Frankl termed it "man's search for meaning," so each one is in search of meaning.[10] As growing persons ministering to growing persons, experience becomes the matrix of ministry—the interrelation of history, perception (and perspective), and even heredity coming together to form unique persons seeking common experiences as a way, perhaps, of knowing and sharing with one another in the uncharted regions of existence called everyday life. For life is certainly uncharted for each pilgrim in search of the Unknown by whom he seeks to be known. The question becomes, "What is the ultimate meaning of my life and where in the world (or in the next world) am I headed?" It becomes extremely threatening to the pilgrim for the tour guide (minister) to admit that he does not know the answer to such a question, and, in fact, is struggling in his own pilgrimage. But, in the unveiling of these struggles, the common ground of ministry is found. Perhaps it is just as threatening, if not more so, for the minister to reckon with his own ambivalence and searchings, in that he does not have the ultimate answers, as he initiates ministry.

Application

1. What is man's highest purpose? Why was it important for man to have free will in order to fulfill this purpose?

2. What decision did man make which resulted in the breakdown of his relationship with God? How did this decision affect his relationships with others?

3. How is anxiety related to sin? Do you think anxiety is a significant factor in the inactivity of your church's dropouts? What

specifically were the causes (that you are aware of) of this anxiety in the lives of these persons?

4. How do you think an inactive member feels about his level of discipleship? How are these feelings expressed?

5. Can you name any members of your church who have become inactive because they are bored or frustrated with the church (either they were not "receiving enough" from the church or the church did not give them the kind of experience they wanted)? Do any of the inactive members of the church see no importance in church since they are already saved and going to heaven?

Notes

1Paul F. Schmidt, *Coping with Difficult People* (Philadelphia: Westminster Press, 1980), p. 18.

2DeVern F. Fromke, *Ultimate Intention* (Mount Vernon: Sure Foundation Publishers, 1962), p. 10, quoted in Raymond C. Ortlund, "Priorities for the Local Church," *Bibliotheca Sacra* 138 (January-March 1981): 7.

3Ortland, "Being the People of God Together," *Bibliotheca Sacra* 138 (July-September 1981): 196.

4W.T. Conner, *Christian Doctrine* (Nashville: Broadman Press, 1937), pp. 259-261.

5Ibid., p. 227.

6Richard A. Hoehn, *Up from Apathy* (Nashville: Abingdon Press, 1983), pp. 16-17.

7Paul Tillich, *The Shaking of the Foundations* (New York: Charles Scribners' Sons, 1948), pp. 104, 106.

8John E. Biersdorf, *Hunger for Experience* (New York: The Seabury Press, 1975), p. 83-96.

9Robert A. Frykholm, "A Relational Theology of the Laity," *The Iliff Review* 37 (Fall 1980), p. 21.

10The title of Frankl's book. Viktor E. Frankl, *Man's Search for Meaning* (New York: Pocket Books, 1973).

6
What Are We to Do About It?

The very fact that such a significant portion of the members of churches today are not active stands as an indictment against us concerning our unwillingness to address the issue of inactivity. What are our responsibilities to our fellow church members? Shall we join in the Cain Chorus and apathetically ask, "Am I my brother's keeper?" or shall we accept our loving obligation to reach out to our fellow members who have dropped out? Why does the church not do more to reclaim its wounded rather than just burying them? These are questions I shall attempt to answer in this chapter.

Be Ye Reconciled

Our preeminent responsibility before God is to be reconciled to those with whom we have fallen out of fellowship. The biblical doctrine of reconciliation points out the inconsistency of professing oneness with God in Christ while maintaining a disunity among believers. Therefore, the doctrine of reconciliation forms an ethical demand for oneness in Christ among believers. It follows that any need for reconciliation with church members, particularly those who have ceased to actively function as a viable part of the church, demands action on the part of the church in rectifying such a problem. The primary model for such action is Jesus Christ. In Ephesians 2, Paul discusses the "enmity" existing between the "Uncircumcision" (Gentiles) and the "Circumcision" (Jews) which was bridged in Christ,

But now in Christ Jesus ye who sometimes were far off are made nigh by the blood of Christ. For he is our peace, who hath made both one, and hath broken down the middle wall of partition between us; Having abolished in his flesh the enmity . . . to make in himself of twain one new man, so making peace; and that he might reconcile both unto God in one body by the cross, having slain the enmity thereby: And came and preached peace to you which were afar off, and to them that were nigh (v. 13-17).

Christ, once making reconciliation between men, also "preached peace." How are believers to preach the peace of God in Christ with integrity when there is not peace in Christ among the brethren? This behooves the church to address the crisis of inactivity as one which lays at the foundation of relationships in Christ.

Reclamation in the New Testament Church

The New Testament church addressed partitions of fellowship that arose within its ranks. By briefly examining New Testament passages dealing with the subject, at least a few models will emerge for addressing fellowship problems in the church today.

Relationships Are Important

Emphasis was placed on unity in the New Testament church as evidenced by several texts. Acts 2:41-47 records the unity of the church upon its inception at Pentecost. In this passage five manifestations of unity in relationships among the early believers are recorded. First, the mode of entrance into the Christian community was baptism (v.41). Second, the authority of the apostles' teaching was recognized (v.42). Third, a *koinonia*-fellowship was seen in the "breaking of bread," the common meal, which later became distinct as communion (vv.42,46). Fourth, the commonality of property was observed (vv.44,45). Fifth, the witness of joy was felt, resulting in the respect of the public and daily conversions (vv.46, 47).[1] Obviously, the problem of inactive membership did not exist at that date!

Many symbols and metaphors are used in the New Testament to emphasize relational unity among believers. For example: vine and branches (John 15), the Lord's Supper,[2] and the cross itself (Eph.

2:16) are used. The church is referred to as a body, building, flock, nation, the assembly, a *koinonia* (fellowship). Do these symbols and metaphors describe your church?

In the New Testament, great emphasis is placed upon forgiveness and tolerance. Since the believer is yet an imperfect being at best, it follows that his imperfection will affect his relationships with others. Therefore, the biblical writers enjoin us to be tolerant of one another in the Christian life.[3]

No doubt there are characteristics and idiosyncrasies in all of us which cause a certain amount of consternation in others. I like *The New English Bible* translation of Philippians 4:5. "Let your magnanimity be manifest to all." Magnanimity is, according to Webster, being "generous in overlooking injury or insult; rising above pettiness." A magnanimous spirit of overlooking the petty differences in people does much to strengthen the fellowship of a church.[4]

Meet the Problem Head On

Another relevant model found in the New Testament is that of addressing problems in the fellowship in a personal encounter, face-to-face. In Acts 6, a problem arose in which the Hellenistic widows felt slighted in the daily distributions. The Greek names of the "committee" members elected to deal with the problem is indicative of the magnanimous spirit present in the church. Significantly, the church confronted the issue head on. This form of addressing the problem directly led to an apparent solution to not only an administrative mix up, but an evidently deeper problem of prejudice as well.

Jesus sets forth confrontational principles of reconciliation in Matthew 5:23-24; 18:15-17, which entail going to a fellow believer to seek reconciliation if he has been offended by you, and to initiate reconciliation with a fellow believer who has offended you. Hebrews 10:24-25 teaches believers to stir up love and good works, not to forsake the assembly, but to exhort one another. James (2:1-9) confronts partiality in the early church with a candid illustration of giving deferential treatment to a rich man attending a service while neglecting the poor man who attends.

It is possible to study the theological implications of ministry and inactivity and then do nothing to initiate reconciliation. Such an approach would be what Guy Greenfield calls, "the heresy of nonrelational theology," which is a "theology that emphasizes ideas to the neglect of relationships."[5] While most of us would not like to be called a heretic, not taking action to reach inactive members is a practical heresy: believing and professing one thing while doing another. Indeed, in this sense, it is challenging to practice orthodox ministry.

Theology that stresses relationships is called "relational theology." Frykholm defines relational theology as

a contemporary faith style which seeks to stimulate personal Christian growth and renewed church vitality by relating believers to one another in settings designed to encourage openness, acceptance, accountability, and specific steps in the exercising of personal faith. It holds up the possibility of finding spiritual life through relationships with other people.[6]

Hindrances to Ministry

All this talk of relationships and reconciliation sounds good, and looks good on paper, but why don't we do it? I believe more ministry would take place in churches if our members really understood what ministry is. Many of the idealistic and ethereal notions people have about ministry are undermined when they find themselves in a real ministry situation. People do not always respond the way we think they should or even the way we expect them to. An inactive member may not be open to a visit. He may avoid contact with his fellow church members. Sometimes people are downright ugly even to well-meaning Christians who are only trying to love them. This can be devastating to naive church members and discouraging to seasoned ministers.

The bottom line of ministry is that two people must get together and have some kind of meaningful communication. Ideas must be exchanged and relationships established. In order for this to occur, someone has to take the initiative—and it won't be the inactive member! That's why we call them "inactive!"

As the member takes initiative and the person, who is the object of ministry, responds, the two come together in what I call the *ministry event.* Several things serve to hinder this process. A helpful way of looking at the ministry process and these hindrances is known as *force field analysis.*

Kurt Lewin defines his theory of force field as, "a method of analyzing causal relations and of building scientific constructs." His theory states that in any conflict situation, or even between any two persons, there are "driving forces" and "restraining forces," as well as neutral forces, at work in the interpersonal relationship.[7] Persons bring to any ministry encounter factors that influence their behavior. This environment, or field, of influences contains hindrances and facilitators of the ministry process.

Christian writers, such as Reuel Howe, have seen the theological implications of force field analysis. Howe speaks of "meaning barriers to communication." One such basic barrier to dialogue, or the "meeting of meaning," is ontological concerns. Ontological concerns refer to one's concern over his own being, as every person is both finite and burdened with a sense of guilt and lives in relation to known and unknown threats to his being.[8]

What does all this have to do with ministry? Ministry can be threatening. The anxiety precipitated by the drawing near to the ministry event can be so profound as to rob the event of any practical meaning and effect. You, or members of your church involved in reclamation ministry, may be very anxious about making visits to inactive members. Fears of the unknown and possible negative encounters serve as a formidable barrier to ministry. These fears are sometimes so great that members will simply not make such visits. Let's face it, it's a part of all of us!

Not only are members sometimes fearful of ministry events but inactive members may shrink back from these encounters as well. A woman who had been inactive for several months was contacted by her church. The caller was greeted by a cordial voice on the telephone but could not make an appointment to see her. She would offer one excuse and then another. Subsequent attempts met with the same fate.

Reclaimers must learn to deal with their own anxiety and the anxiety of dropouts as well if any ministry is to take place. How can they do this?

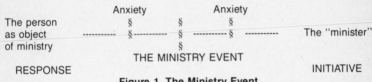

Figure 1. The Ministry Event

In the Figure 1 diagram, the process of ministry and the barriers of anxiety are illustrated. The minister (whether pastor or church member) may take initiative in ministry, but there has to be a concomitant response from the object of ministry. As minister and the object of ministry come together in a meeting halfway, there are impediments to this process on both sides: things that keep both from getting to that point of contact effectively. Many of these hindrances have to do with anxiety. This anxiety absorbs energies, causes a focusing on self, and makes the minister performance-minded. This emotional baggage detracts from the ministry process.

Unfortunately, anxiety is not the only barrier to ministry. Perceptions differ. The inactive member may think of his problem in one way and the reclaimer in another. In fact, there may be big differences in how the two persons view life itself, much more the Christian life. Each person has his own background and history of experience that shapes his perception of things.

Negative experiences are sometimes extrapolated onto other experiences. After being rejected for a church staff position due to his history of marital problems, a member became inactive. He had come to believe that the members of his church looked down upon him and his wife. He could not worship with those by whom he felt condemned. Members have the task of bridging these perceptual barriers that exist between the inactive member and themselves. How can they do this?

What you may be expecting and even hoping to read at this point are steps on how to overcome these barriers. Perhaps you wish there were pat answers to these perplexing dilemmas. I could elaborate on some psychological theories and enumerate three steps to take to solve these problems, but they would only be patent medicine. I will offer some practical suggestions in overcoming these barriers in chapter 9. There is only one real answer, however. A force greater than the anxiety and meaning barriers exists which can make it possible to reclaim members in the worst of circumstances. In fact, it is the only explainable factor in reclamation which makes a difference in the behavior of inactive members. No explanation can be offered as to why the telephone calls and visits have a reclaiming effect apart from this factor. Without this element, all the techniques and suggestions are vain. It is Christian love. The reality of love expressed and reciprocated in ministry encounters is the one decisive factor. Something more than telephone surveys and living room chats must take place if members are to be restored to the life and work of the church. Relationships must be forged. As one preacher concluded in a sermon entitled "Love is Stronger Than Death:"

> Love overcomes separation and creates participation in which there is more than that which the individuals involved can bring to it. Love is the infinite which is given to the finite. Therefore we love in others, for we do not merely love others, but we love the Love that is in them and which is more than their or our love. In mutual assistance that which is most important is not the alleviation of need but the actualization of love. Of course, there is no love which does not want to make the other's need its own. But there is also no true help which does not spring from love and create love.[9]

Biblically, love is the dynamic of true Christian ministry. In the words of Christ, "By this all men will know that you are my disciples, if you have love for one another" (John 13:35, RSV). Paul's commentary on Proverbs 10:12, "love covers all sins," comprises the heart of the "love chapter" of his letter to the strife-torn, factious Corinthian church:

> Love suffers long and is kind; love does not envy; love does not parade itself, is not puffed up; does not behave rudely, does not seek its own, is not provoked, thinks no evil; does not rejoice in iniquity, but rejoices in the truth; bears all things, believes all things, hopes all things, endures all things. Love never fails (1 Cor. 13:4-8, NJKV).

May you go forth in the love of Christ to restore those hurting and straying ones to the fold of Christian fellowship and worship. As Jesus loves us in spite of our rough edges, may we love our sisters and brothers in Christ, looking beyond the exteriors of harshness which sometime alienate one from another to see precious souls for which Christ died.

Application

1. What are the obligations of the church in ministering to inactive members? Why is it possible for inactive members to be reclaimed?

2. What two things mentioned in this chapter did the New Testament church do to maintain the fellowship?

3. Why is unity in the church important? Why is it crucial to take direct action in dealing with problems in the church between members?

4. Several hindrances to ministry were discussed in this chapter, can you recognize any of these barriers in your church?

Notes

[1]E.M. Blaiklock, *The Acts of the Apostles,* Tyndale New Testament Commentaries, No. 5 (Grand Rapids: Wm. B. Eerdmans Publishing Company, 1976), pp. 61-62.

[2]Referred to as the "love feasts" by the early church, as discussed in *The Interpreter's Dictionary of the Bible,* 1962 ed., s.v. "Agape, The", by M.H. Shepherd, Jr. Shepherd's article, s.v. "Lord's Supper, The," in the above work, points out that the problems with factions in the Corinthian church confronted by Paul as dealt with in conjunction with communion (1 Cor. 11:17-34) reveal the Lord's Supper as a relational symbol.

[3]Such as Ephesians 4:2-3, "With all lowliness and gentleness, with longsuffering, bearing with one another in love, endeavoring to keep the unity of the Spirit in the bond of peace"; Philippians 4:5, "Let your gentleness be known to all men"; and Colossians 3:13, "bearing with one another, and forgiving one another, if anyone has a complaint against another; even as Christ forgave you, so you also must do" (NKJV).

[4]Jones, "A Neglected Ministry, Reclaiming," pp. 7-8.

[5]Guy Greenfield, *We Need Each Other* (Grand Rapids: Baker Book House, 1984), p. 16.,

[6]Frykholm, "A Relational Theology of the Laity," pp. 13-14.

[7]Kurt Lewin, *Field Theory in Social Science* (New York: Harper and Brothers Publisher, 1951), pp. 33-59.

[8]Reuel L. Howe, *The Miracle of Dialogue* (New York: The Seabury Press, 1963), pp. 3-69.

[9]Paul Tillich, *The New Being* (New York: Charles Scribner's Sons, 1955), p. 173.

III
Methods for Reclaiming

When I was in college I came down to my very last semester needing one semester hour of biology! My degree plan required twelve hours of biology. I had taken two four-hour courses and a three-hour course. Now I realized the error of my ways! I wanted so desperately to graduate that semester, get married in the summer, and begin seminary the next fall. All my plans were naught if I didn't earn that one hour of biology. So, I enrolled in the only biology course I could get into: a three-hour advanced genetics course.

I can still remember the first day of class. The first thing the professor said was that if any of the students in the class were not biology majors, then they should get out immediately. This was an advanced course in genetics. As I sank in my seat, I resigned myself to the ensuing struggle to pass genetics. It was a nightmare! I passed—by the genetically designed skin of my teeth! I studied hard, and yet still couldn't answer many of the test questions correctly. The reason: I didn't have the prerequisite courses.

If you read books like I do you, this may be the first page you are reading of this book. I like to skip past the theoretical and jump straight into the practical. When I look at the contents, I look for the chapters that tell me how to do the thing I bought the book to learn how to do. So, welcome to the practical section!

Seriously, it doesn't much matter to me which part of the book you start with as long as you read each part! If you are starting with this section, let me urge you to go back and pick up the rest of the chapters before you try to implement any of the suggestions of this book. I make no guarantees about the ministry of reclamation outlined in this book except to guarantee that it will flop wholeheartedly if you attempt this ministry without the foundation established in the previous chapters.

An effective methodology for reclaiming inactive members must have at least three components: definition, identification, and mobilization. These three components of reclamation are broad sections of the overall process. Many traditional approaches to reclaiming are less than effective because they omit necessary steps in reaching the inactive member. The purpose of this section is to set forth sound principles of reclamation methodology. The three chapters of this section, show specifically what inactivity is, how to identify the inactive members of your church, and how to mobilize your church to reclaim the drop outs.

I will outline a program of ministry to implement in your church. There will be specific suggestions and a choice of options. It is up to you to fit the program to the needs of your congregation.[1]

Notes

[1]For information about workshops and consultation by the author, write to the author at Reclamation Workshops, 5041 Glade St., Fort Worth, TX 76114.

7
Defining the Process of Inactivity

My wife and I love to vacation in a certain Southwestern city. One of the attractions of this city is a beautiful botanical park called The Japanese Gardens. We visited these gardens on our honeymoon. Back then they were called The Chinese Gardens. Why the name change? Actually, the gardens were originally called The Japanese Gardens. After the attack of the Japanese on our Navy port at Pearl Harbor, the name was changed to The Chinese Gardens. Many Americans in those days despised the Japanese for that attack, and consequently it was felt that people would not want to visit a park named after the Japanese. It is a commentary on the current good relations between our two countries that the name of this park has been restored. Good motives abound where ill will once flourished.

As pointed out in the introduction, our attitude toward inactive members will strongly influence our actions toward them. If we see inactive members as mere dead wood, we will simply want to clear them off the rolls. However, if we view the dropouts of our church as persons of worth with real needs, we will adopt a different stance toward them. I know that your heart must beat with the same burden for souls as mine. Let's reclaim the inactive members to the fellowship of our churches and to renewed usefulness in the kingdom of God!

What Does It Mean to Be Active?

Get out the definition of inactivity that you worked up earlier. Ask yourself three questions about your definition. *First, is it workable?* Will it work? Is it practical? Are you defining inactivity in such a way that you can later go back and minister to these people? One definition I saw in a church's constitution and bylaws was ambiguous. As a result, it was very difficult to know who was technically active or not. Another problem with that definition was that by the time a person fulfilled the requirement for being an inactive member, they were long gone from the church. It was impractical to try to reclaim a member who had been inactive for five years. Most of them could not even be found, much less ministered to!

Second, is your definition measurable? How do you know if the person is inactive or not? On the basis of your definition, can you determine how many inactive members you have and who they are? Will your definition allow you to know when you have actually reclaimed them? There needs to be no confusion about this!

Third, is your definition understandable? The more simple it is the better. Yet, the definition needs to be encompassing. If your definition was read from the pulpit this Sunday, would everyone understand it?

With all this in mind, look at an example of a definition of inactivity:

"An inactive member is a resident member of the church who has ceased to participate in the life and work of the church as evidenced by a lack of attendance and financial support or who has shown a marked decrease in such participation to the point that this participation is minimal.

Look at this definition more closely. Compare it to yours. Your definition may be superior to this one, but a good definition is the necessary starting point in reclamation. In fact, it is so important that it deserves a detailed look.

". . . a resident member of the church . . ."

A member who no longer resides within the community of the church is not an inactive member, he is a nonresident member. At times you will find even active members of the church who live outside the community. Perhaps they once lived near the church and later moved away. Yet, they continue to attend and/or contribute to the church. The church I serve has many such members. Our church is celebrating its seventy-fifth anniversary. Over the years, many persons have grown up in the church, gotten married, raised a family, and even retired while remaining an active member of the church. They may have even changed residences. Some of our folks have moved out of the almost downtown neighborhood of our church to the suburbs and beyond.

How far can a member live from the church and still be active? This depends a great deal on the faithfulness and commitment of the member. I know of one family who lived thirty miles from the church and attended every Sunday morning. But, that was the extent of their attendance. They found it hard to attend any of the other services or functions. When their children reached youth, they sensed the need for a greater involvement in a local church and changed membership.

A couple in the church moved to the country after retirement. Having grown up in the church and being a part of the fellowship for all those many years, they could not bring themselves to join the church near their home. They send in their tithes and offerings regularly and attend seldom.

It is my opinion that when a member lives more than a comfortable driving distance away from the church—more than they would regularly want to drive to all the services they would otherwise attend—they are living too far from the church to really be active. It would be unreasonable for the church to expect them to be fully active, and it would be just as unreasonable for them to expect the church to have a full ministry to them. That's a decision they have made upon moving so far away. No pastor, unless in a pioneer area where the church field covers a large territory, should feel obligated to provide the kind of ministry to these members as he does to those in the church field.

Serious questions arise concerning the discipleship and commitment of members who maintain membership in a church so far away that they cannot be fully active. Reclamation ministry to such members may well entail the encouragement to unite with a local church wherein they can serve and be served most effectively.

". . . who has ceased to participate in the
life and work of the church as evidenced by
a lack of attendance and financial support . . ."

How can one describe, behaviorally, when a person becomes an inactive member? The crux is to get at that juncture when a person changes from active to inactive. The problem is that this is not always a definite point in time. A person may become sporadic in attendance before finally dropping out. For others, there is a definite cutoff point.

One might expect a definition to include a certain time frame, such as "not attending church for twelve months." It might be necessary to set a time criterion for the purposes of defining members as active in the church bylaws, but such a time frame would be detrimental to a ministry of reclaiming. To wait twelve months before deciding that a member is inactive is too long. It has been found that persons who have been inactive for more than six to eight weeks are increasingly difficult to reclaim. Therefore, the definition of inactivity for such a ministry must be a process definition which sees members as taking steps out of the realm of active participation. The further the process progresses, the harder it is to reverse.

In order to define inactivity, one must define activity. What is an active church member? Activity may involve a host of elements and behaviors, such as prays for the needs of fellow members, studies Sunday School lesson, attends services and other church functions, drives the church bus, brings fruit salad to church socials, plays an instrument in worship, passes the offering plate, donates money to the church, or sings in the choir. It would be impossible to know everything a member does or feels which is involved in active churchmanship.

Of all the behaviors associated with active participation in a local church, at least two are essential: attendance and financial contribution. If a person neither attends services or other activities nor contributes financially to the church, one would be hard pressed to show that this person is active. This can be supported biblically.

"Not forsaking the assembling of ourselves together," (Heb. 10:25) is the oft quoted verse used to teach the obligation of the believer to attend church. That the meaning of the verse includes church attendance is indisputable. The Greek word translated "assembling" in this verse is *episunagoge,* meaning a "gathering together beyond." Some commentators see this as a reference to the meeting of the Jewish Christians other than at the synagogue. In this sense, it would mean "beyond synagogue." In the context, the writer is encouraging his Jewish Christian readers not to revert to the Judaism out of which they had been saved but to continue in the Christian faith and the local gatherings of the believers. By remaining faithful in church attendance, the believers were identifying with the faith of Christ. And so it is today!

In regards to financial contributions, Paul relates the financial support of the Philippian church to the "fellowship of the gospel" (2 Cor. 8:4; Phil. 1:5; 4:15). Giving was, to him, an integral way in which these believers manifested their Christian fellowship *(koinonia),* thus evidencing their participation in the ministry of the church.

These two behaviors, attendance and contributions, are appropriate indicators of activity in a local church because they are measurable. Most churches keep attendance and contribution records. These behaviors are indicators of activity; they can be indicators of inactivity as well.

**". . . or who has shown a marked decrease
in such participation to the point that this
participation is minimal."**

This last phrase in the definition is needed to emphasize the fact that inactivity is a process. For the purpose of ministry, we are interested in knowing that a person is in the process of becoming inactive.

Mrs. Brown has missed three Sundays in a row. She may be in trouble! A contact may reveal that she has been out of town, moved, sick, or is upset with the church. If you wait until it is clearly obvious that she is inactive, then you have forfeited your best opportunity to reclaim her!

Here the need for constant monitoring of these two indicators of activity, attendance and contributions, becomes apparent. The next chapter will explain how to effectively track the members of your church and spot these dropouts before they drop out! But first, in order to illustrate the various ways the process of inactivity is lived out by members, let me share with you some of the most common routes of departure I've observed.

The Inactivity Games People Play

If you've ever gone to a ball game with an avid fan, you know that some people take their sports seriously. In the same way, issues that may seem petty to you are of great importance to some of the members of your church. It looks like they're playing, but they are for real! You'd better learn the rules of their games or they'll soon be sitting in the bleachers! Have you ever been invited to play in any of these games?

Hide and Seek, "Come and Get Me!"

Before you know it, they're gone. They didn't say anything about being unhappy, but they are. You were busy or preoccupied with things or certain people, and they slipped out right under your nose. Don't expect a call announcing their inactivity, either.

They are sitting at home on Sunday waiting for someone down at the church to notice their absence and care enough to contact them. "This is the only way I'll know if those people at that church really care about me or not!" they say to themselves when the haunting feelings overtake them. They fear, whether they would ever admit it or not, that just maybe those people down at the church don't care.

One thing is very clear. According to the rules of this game, if someone from the church doesn't call out "Ready or not, here I come!" pretty soon, these dropouts will have made up their minds about the church. Learn to read the very subtle signs these members give that they are about to scurry for cover. Help them to express their feelings before they sense the need to call another "Duck and Cover" drill!

Often members will give you a few clues as to their intentions of dropping out. They will first begin to skip Sunday School or other small group participation. Next, they will begin to be absent from worship. Finally, their offerings are stopped. These actions are their ways of crying out, "Come and get me!"

Charades, "Can You Figure Out What My Actions Mean?"

"Jim sure has been acting strange lately." Its Charades! Only its a serious game. Jim doesn't know how to just come right out and say that he is hurt—or he finds it very hard to admit it—so he acts out his pain. He's trying to get your attention with those subtle and cloaked remarks about the upcoming business meeting or the boss wanting him to start working on Sundays. What's your reaction? Will you guess the message he's trying to communicate?

Your member is sending out a message for help. He's hurting! He has been offended or embarrassed. Perhaps he just can't agree with something that has been decided. He feels overlooked or underrated.

Jim opts for Charades because of his insecurity in revealing his true thoughts and feelings. Can he find acceptance if other members really see him as he is? Time will give you opportunities to affirm his attempts at authentic communication. As Jim's trust in your acceptance grows, so will his straight-forwardness.

The Merry-Go-Round, "Its Me Again!"

How many times have you been through this with Sharon? A dozen times? Its the same old story. She'll show up at the church one Sunday like everything's fine. You'd think she was a pillar of the church the way she speaks up about things. Never mind the fact that no one has seen her in church for two months. You can count on her coming for two or three consecutive Sundays and then she's out again. Wonder if she'll grab the brass ring this time around?

This type of player may also like to "ride the roller coaster." There are the high times of commitment and enthusiasm and the low times of discouragement and apathy. Further investigation may reveal a person who is overly dependent on circumstances for their sense of well-being. Their contentment in life is fixed upon the rising and falling tides of unrelated factors in life. They have grown accustomed to using emotions as their chief means of motivation. Emotions are fickle, though, and so they become unstable and unreliable. Help them learn to see beyond the immediate crisis or victory to a broader view of life. Encourage their efforts to press on when their feelings lag.

The Fast Ball, "Three Strikes, You're Out!"

What you didn't know about Bill was that he was just waiting for one more reason to drop out. Last week he told his wife, "If they have another council meeting without calling me again, I'm out of there! I'm tired of being treated like a nobody. I've got just as much a right to my opinion as anybody else!" Your church had two strikes against it and you didn't even know you were at bat. Sure enough, when nobody called Bill about the regularly scheduled council meeting, that was the last strike. You're out, and so is Bill!

Sometimes it is worthwhile to accommodate the hardball players in your church. Their input and participation may be an asset worth preserving. But, also be aware that the other two strikes may not have been by you or your church. You are being treated unfairly as a result of this member's frustrations from other sources. Helping him cope with his stresses may save the game for your church!

Poker Player's Bluff, "I Am Going to . . ."

Sometimes known as the ultimatum game, a member lets others know in advance what his actions are going to be if certain things do or do not happen. Sometimes the stakes are pretty high as a member ignorantly backs himself into a corner. If the person doesn't deliver on his promise, soon he loses all credibility and becomes like the boy who cried "wolf!" If he does live up to his threat, the price may be higher than he wanted to pay in terms of the broken relationships that ensue.

It is tempting to spout off with ultimatums when an important issue is about to be decided. "If the church cuts the missions budget, I'm leaving." "If they don't get rid of that staff member, I'm going to look for another church." "If they change the time for the evening service,

I'll just have to miss it from now on." "I'll designate all my offerings for the youth budget if they don't pay the kids' way to camp!" The big "ifs" are wielded like a weapon.

What a person is really saying with an ultimatum is that a particular issue is so important that he is willing to cash in all his chips for it. Below the surface, however, he is saying "If I'm important to you, you'll go along with me rather than risk losing me." It becomes a sort of ecclesiastical extortion.

The bluff is designed only to get your attention. The person really doesn't want to leave but desperately wants to change things or influence an outcome. The motives may even be noble. But, the affect is the same: the church is put on notice.

Dealing with your poker-faced members requires tact and directness. If you back down now, you'll be bluffed again and again. Church members will soon grow to resent the extortionist in their midst, and the scheme backfires. Sooner or later the risk-taker is going to have to learn that when he crawls out on a limb it just might break. The dangerous thing about ultimatums is that sometimes people call your bluff!

Cowboys and Indians, "Us . . . and Them"

"Bang, you're dead!" "No I'm not!" "Yes you are, I shot you with my bow and arrow!" "No you didn't, I nuked you first!" So goes the modern version of Cowboys and Indians being played by neighborhood children. The battle has spilled over into what's left of my front yard after an assortment of thermonuclear exchanges and laser fire.

One of the most hurtful and destructive inactivity games is any variety of war games people play in church. Enter: some divisive or controversial issue, even if it has to be created. Exit: the losers. It is all too common for congregations to settle some issue by posturing themselves into a win-lose stance. The winners take all; the rest leave or lose face.

A dead giveaway that members are playing this game is their choice of pronouns when referring to other members. "They" are the misguided, foolish, erroneous members who are on the wrong side of an issue. "We" are the fellows of kindred spirit who are aligned against "them."

First Country Church had voted to purchase a new piano for the sanctuary. Soon the church was embroiled in debate over which side of the platform to place the new instrument. "The piano goes on the left so the sound board will open towards the audience," claimed a choir member. "The piano has always been on the right side," countered the chairman of the music committee, whose committee was evenly divided on the subject. It was member against member, deacon against deacon, and staff member against staff member. Even families were divided. Finally a special meeting was called to decide by a vote of the church. The center isle was like a demilitarized zone. The right-siders sat on the right, the left-siders on the left. As the heated discussion drew to a close and the time for voting approached, one elderly gentlemen stood and called to the other side, "Honey, now which side was it I wanted the piano?"

Defuse the warriors in your church by deferring the issue to a later time when more information will be available, offering a compromise with integrity, or delegating the decision to a neutral and qualified party.

8
Identifying Inactive Members

The church record-keeping system is a crucial element in the ministry of reclamation. It is important to have data concerning the attendance and contributions of members in order to monitor their activity. I call this *tracking* the members.

In my church, for example, we record actual attendance. A person may attend four times a week (Sunday School, Sunday morning and evening worship, and Wednesday evening worship). If attendance is recorded as only once per week for all services, the data can be misleading. Should a person who consistently attends every service begin to drop out of some of the services, this type of record system would not signal the decline in activity.

Allan had a confrontation with the choir leader over the choice for the Christian musical. Allen felt the classical selection of the director would not appeal to most of the members of the congregation and approached the leader after rehearsal. "We are not here for a talent show to see what the people like the most. Our church needs to learn to appreciate the finer works of sacred music!" shot back the music minister. Allen felt humiliated and angry. Allen dropped out of choir and quit attending the Wednesday evening rehearsals. In fact, he no longer attended the Wednesday evening services.

Contributions are recorded by each week (they either contributed once or none that week). Most church members are very sensitive about the confidentiality of their records, particularly contributions. The figure that is important here is not so much the amount of contributions as the frequency. Different members give differently.

Even if all tithe, the amount of the tithes would vary with the amount of income. The frequency of contributions, however, is significant. Here again, there is much variety and a single criterion for frequency of contributions cannot be established for all members.

The Jacksons are consistent contributors to the church and give their tithe on the first Sunday of every month because they are paid monthly. Conversely, some members may give every week putting a dollar bill in the plate at every service, but do not give even one percent of their income.

Without entering into undue controversy over contribution records, the frequency of gifts can be used as one way to measure the activity of a member. Any change in the pattern of frequency will signal a change in the level of activity.

Where Did All the People Go?

As I was handed the attendance register while visiting Parksville Memorial Church, It occured to me that some churches have a definite advantage when it comes to tracking the attendance of members. At Parksville, members register their attendance at the worship service. This is done with register cards in the pew. Recently this large church issued nicely made name tags for all its members. These tags have the logo of the church and the member's name printed on them. They are arranged alphabetically on boards at major entrances to the building (where a particular member enters most often). Worshipers simply drop their tags into boxes at the doors on their way out of the building. In churches that have not historically registered worshipers, this might be difficult to implement. But, attendance at worship is crucial information for reclamation.

If your church does not register worshipers, you might consider these options. Grace Church is a small urban congregation. Their means of tracking attendance is to have persons assigned to register attendance. This is done by the ushers and staff members. The pastor even does this by looking over the church roll right after the service while his memory is still fresh. The attendance records are then supplemented by the visitor's cards filled out by visitors during the service. At best, it is a tedious process, and requires consistency and faithfulness on the part of those responsible. But, it is a workable system.

Trinity Community Church keeps worship attendance records by passing registers down the pews at a certain point in the service. In this way, visitors and members alike are registered. One major drawback of this approach, however, is that it may disrupt the flow of worship.

St. John's Church has found that attendance at Bible study classes is generally much easier to record. Most churches already have a system similar to St. John's of recording Bible study, or Sunday School, attendance. A class secretary keeps the records and turns them in to the general secretary where overall records are maintained. With the advent of computerized attendance records, this process has been improved greatly, requiring less time and effort.

At St. John's Church the attendance and contribution records are compiled and examined each week using a master record form. The form was devised to list each member alphabetically and show each week's attendance and contribution record. This method for compiling attendance and contribution records makes it easy to spot dropout patterns. Figure 2 is an example of the master form. A place is provided on the left for the name of the member with places across the page to record each week's records for fifty-three weeks (only eight weeks are shown here). After each month a column displays the monthly totals so that monthly figures can be compared. Over to the

Name	Attendance/Contributions									
Week:	1	2	3	4	Total	5	6	7	8	Total
John Doerg	3/1	4/0	2/1	1/0	10/2	1/1	1/0	0/0	0/0	2/1
Marj Effort	4/1	4/1	3/1	4/1	15/4	3/1	4/1	3/1	4/1	14/4
	/	/	/	/	/	/	/	/	/	/
	/	/	/	/	/	/	/	/	/	/
Totals:	7/2	8/1	5/2	5/1	25/6	4/2	5/1	3/1	4/1	16/5

Figure 2. The Master Form

far right (not shown) is a column for a grand total for the whole year. Shown here are only two members' records. Notice that one has become inactive!

At this point, the most important piece of data obtained is the pattern of activity. Church leaders can compare current levels of attendance and number of contributions with the recent past, and can see when a person is becoming inactive as he becomes inactive.

Other forms of data are obtained from the master form that are helpful such as statistical analyses of the records to determine averages and totals. The average rate of activity can easily be determined by dividing the bottom row of totals by the number of members. In the example given, the average attendance for the first month was 12.5 (25 divided by 2). This statistic allows one to quickly spot those members who are below average in attendance. By comparing monthly totals, the cause for any decline in attendance could be directly linked to specific individuals. In this example, the reason for the decline between the first and second month is because of John Doerg's inactivity in the second month.

All of this record keeping and tabulating requires a lot of work. Some churches could assign this task to a paid secretary, while St. John's depends upon a volunteer who really wants to see the dropouts reached.

Upon implementing a system of tracking their members' activity, St. John's was unpleasantly surprised. For once they could see on paper the activity patterns of their members. The problem of inactivity was glaring.

Of course, even the most complete and detailed information is worthless if it is not appropriated by persons who will put it to good use. This information is studied confidentially in weekly staff meetings, deacons meetings, and weekly Sunday School workers meetings. At that point appropriate action is discussed and initiated.

Who Are the Inactive Members of Your Church?

The time has come to begin the ministry of reclamation in your church! Now that you understand the nature of inactivity and have definite ideas about discovering the dropouts of your church, it is time to go to work. The following step-by-step plan can be used to make an initial assessment of the inactivity problem of your church.

Obtain the Necessary Information

If your church is small enough, this could be done in the pastor's office. You will need an up-to-date roll of the resident members of your church. A recent directory may be used.

You will also need the records from your Sunday School. Each class should have a membership roster with attendance posted for each Sunday. If possible, contact the church treasurer or business secretary for information about the number of contributions for each member.

If you have a good memory and your church is small enough, you may be able to remember the worship attendance of each member over the past four weeks. It is not as hard as it sounds. As you look down the roll of members, write down the number of worship services that person has attended. Then add this figure to the number of times the person has attended Sunday School. For example, Mrs. Johnson has attended the morning worship services every Sunday, except last week when she was ill. Upon checking the Sunday School records it was discovered that the only Sunday she attended class was two weeks ago. The treasurer's records indicate that her regular monthly check was received.

After a somewhat long and tedious process of compiling statistics for each member, you will have what is called a base line. A base line is the starting place for analyzing data. It represents the current state of affairs and gives you something with which to compare future data.

If your church is large to the point that it would be impossible to remember the worship attendance of each member and you do not register worshipers, you will have to set up a workable system for record keeping and start collecting base line data over the next four weeks.

Compare the Data

After collecting base line data, compile data for another four weeks. Once you have the base line data and records for an additional four weeks, you are ready to spot your dropouts. Even while collecting base line data you may have noticed some members who were becoming inactive. Do not wait an additional four weeks before reaching out to them! Contact them and see what the problem is. Begin to minister to them immediately.

List the Names of Inactive Members

Two lists of members will be compiled from the records you now have. One, a list of totally inactive members. These members showed no activity whatsoever over the entire eight weeks. Two, a list of members who are becoming inactive. These are members who began dropping out during the eight-week period or the last four-week period.

The results of this study will reveal the extent of your problem. If you find that less than 10 percent of your resident members are inactive, you either have a very new church or a very unusual fellowship! Generally, the older the church the more inactive members will be accumulated over the years.

If you find that 10 to 30 percent of your resident members are inactive, your church is about average or better. You have a significant problem, but so do most other churches! If you find that an even greater percentage of your members are inactive and that many others are in the process of becoming inactive, then you've got a crisis on your hands! You need to finish this book and go to work on this today!

Before you do go to work on reclaiming these inactive members, pray. You are about to enter into God's work in the lives of these persons. It is only as a result of His work that they will ever be truly active again. For some of these members, you will have to wait upon the Spirit of God before you will have a real opportunity to minister to them. Look at each name and ask God to give you a loving spirit for each one. Until you can come to see these people as hurting, needful persons, you are not ready to minister to them.

As you prayerfully examine the list of inactive members of your church, make notes about each one. Are they playing any of the games described in the previous chapter? Are there any circumstances about their lives that you are aware of?

9
Mobilizing for Ministry

This chapter deals with approaches for reclaiming inactive members. One or more of the approaches may be suited for your church situation. By adapting these approaches, or creating your own, you can arrive at a workable method for reclamation.

Essential Elements of Effective Approaches

As a young and not always wise associate pastor, I was out in the neighborhood visiting prospects for the church. Jim, a fellow church member of about the same age, was accompanying me. It was a warm summer afternoon as we walked up the sidewalk and knocked on the screen door. A growling voice of an obviously inebriated man responded. Not being able to see inside while standing in the bright sunlight, I leaned close to the door and introduced myself and companion. Hearing a mumbled and threatening reply, I turned around to find Jim sitting in the car!

For any approach to reclaim inactive members to be successful, certain key ingredients must be present. First, there must be the right kind of people involved. The greatest resource for reclamation ministry is the committed and compassionate members of your church. But, not every committed and compassionate member is suited for this ministry. The rigors of reclamation require that these members be nondefensive in the face of antagonism. They must have the self-confidence and courage to initiate ministry with persons who feel alienated from and perhaps even hostile toward the church.

A chief characteristic of persons who are effective in reclamation is their ability to listen. The lecture approach is definitely inappropriate for this ministry. If you have a member who tends to back people up against a wall and preach in their faces, be sure to train them in more effective ways of ministry. They will only contribute more inactive members to the bunch you already have.

The ability to listen is so important that you will need to spend deliberate time training people in the art of listening.

A second essential element in reclamation is the tracking and identification of inactive members. Some suggestions for tracking and identification have already been outlined. In fact, by now you should have a pretty good idea who the inactive members of your church are.

Third, a workable means of contacting the inactive members must be devised. Several contacts will need to be made. This will require several weeks, if not months. Persons involved in the ministry will need encouragement and inspiration, for results are seldom immediate.

For months Elaine had been asking me to visit her son Frankie. This aging woman was desperately concerned about her son and his family, who had dropped completely out of church. For months I had been visiting Frankie. He was pleasant enough when I came by and always engaged me in some serious philosophical and theological discussion.

Frankie repeatedly declined my invitations to get back into church by saying, "When I'm ready, I'll come, and I'm just not ready." With his statement of decline was usually a hint of a sense of guilt over some sinful tendencies that he never fully expounded upon.

Finally, one Sunday, Frankie did attend the morning worship service! During the invitation he came to the altar and exclaimed, "I'm ready!" At the time, I wondered if all my theological wrangling and explaining the gospel had eventually paid off. Now, I'm sure Frankie's reclamation had more to do with my consistent cultivation of his trust and friendship.

Fourth, in order to maintain an effective program, thorough evaluation must take place at each step. Are you accomplishing what you set out to do? If not, why? How will you improve the program?

First Church of Millersville initiated a grand outreach program involving a telephone survey of the community. Several workers in the church were recruited and the survey taken. The church leadership felt great about the number of members willing to participate in the program and the hundreds of calls made. It was a noble effort with little tangible results. Two persons visited the church on one Sunday as a result of the survey but were not reached for membership.

Apparently, many of the programs maintained by churches today are largely ineffective in accomplishing their purposes. Yet, the programs are continued due to tradition or lack of awareness of their ineffectiveness. Such is the case for many programs designed to reclaim inactive members. So long as no real evaluation is done of ministry, persons involved may be satisfied with their erroneous perceptions of success.

Finally, a truly successful approach to reclamation must be ongoing. Since inactive members were once active, it follows that some of the members of your church who are now active will one day be inactive. How will you reach them during those crucial early weeks of their inactivity without a continuous, ongoing program?

Another reason reclamation programs need to be ongoing is that most, if not all, of the persons reclaimed will have to be reclaimed again. No one-time project can change the disposition and personalities of persons. Reclamation ministry requires long periods of time and consistent, loving effort.

Jack was an example of a reclamation project. He had completely dropped out of church and was voicing some fairly significant emotional and theological problems with the church. Through the competent efforts of Marilyn and Bill, a couple involved in the project who were willing to make several in-depth visits, Jack became very active in the church again. Marilyn and Bill have since moved away.

During a business session at the church, Jack voiced his conviction that the church spend more for social ministry. Apparently frustrated over the congregation's fiscal conservatism, Jack has dropped out again. Unfortunately for Jack and the church, there is no ongoing reclamation ministry and no Marilyn and Bill to reclaim him.

Training the Workers

As you prayerfully recruit workers who are suited for the ministry of reclamation, it will be important to obtain a formal agreement from them. I have found that when persons are asked to do something, have the task properly explained to them, and are asked to make a formal commitment to the task, they are much more likely to follow through with it. Consider having your ministry group members sign a commitment like this.

MINISTRY AGREEMENT

I agree to the following conditions in making a commitment to minister to the inactive members of our church.

1. Attend all training and report sessions for the quarter.

2. Complete all assignments on date due.

3. Learn a special interview process for communicating with inactive members.

4. Participate in group discussions and seek to contribute creative ideas for ministry to inactive members.

5. Survey by phone several inactive members.

6. Make approximately four to six visits each to several inactive members.

7. Time required will be approximately two to four hours a week.

Signed _____

Date   _____

The more the group members know about the process of inactivity, the more effective they will be in ministry. A suggested outline to use in training the group is given in Appendix A. Use the material presented in the previous chapters to "flesh out" the outline. The outline could be reproduced and given to the group for discussion.

Learning to Listen

The development of listening skills is crucial to reclamation. Some exercises in listening will serve to enhance the group members' ability to listen as well as help them deal with their own anxiety about

interviewing inactive members. Two helpful resources for developing
listening skills are: *Helping Skills: A Basic Training Program,* by
Stephen J. Danish and Allen L. Hauer (New York: Human Science
Press, 1977) and *The Helping Interview,* by Alfred Benjamin (Dallas:
Houghton Mifflin Company, 1974). Some insights from these two
books follow.

An effective exercise is to role-play a situation in which the member
is calling or visiting the inactive member. Divide the group into triads.
Each person will take turns in these roles: the calling member, the
inactive member, and the observer. The following procedure is recommended for interviewing inactive members. The observer in each
group could use this procedure as a guide for evaluating the role-play
interview.

Be Prepared to Deal with Resistance

As the ministry group interacts with inactive members, they are
likely to face resistance from the member to the ministry encounter.
Latent hostility may also be triggered by the contact. The ministry
group members must be able to persevere in their contact beyond
these initial barriers toward the establishment of a trust relationship.
There are some things the reclaimers can do to maximize their effectiveness in these encounters.

Entrance can be established by appointment. If the inactive members have prior knowledge of the visit, they will have time to prepare
themselves. An impromptu visit holds the possibility of disastrous
results by catching the member at an inappropriate time. The group
should be encouraged to make an appointment with the member by
telephone before attempting the visit. If the member turned out to be
unreceptive, bad experiences could be forestalled as the member could
more graciously decline the visit over the telephone than if the visitor
were standing on his porch. Furthermore, only members who indicate
a willingness to be contacted further during an initial telephone survey
should be assigned for visitation. This will help to reduce the possibility of negative encounters as well as allow the reclaimers to focus their
time and effort on those more receptive to their ministry.

Deal with initial anxiety by getting to know the inactive members.
Both the group member and the inactive member will have a certain
amount of anxiety about the visit. It would be helpful to begin with
initial conversation to break the ice. An acrostic can be used to help
group members remember an easy formula for making initial conversation: F.O.R.M. (family, occupation, religious background, and message). This is an adaptation of the acrostic used in many evangelistic
training programs. The group member could lead the conversation to
a discussion of the inactive member's family, occupation, church
background (especially your church), and then to statements of encouragement to return to church or to dealing with issues in the
member's inactivity.

The ministry group needs to be equipped as listeners. Several times
throughout the course of the ministry, emphasize that the group is
"ministering with our ears." Schaller points out the need for competent listening in his delineation of the assumptions necessary for an
effective reclamation ministry:

> We assume that we can learn more by listening than by talking, and
> therefore our approach to our inactive members will be one of active
> listening. We can expect this to require at least several hours of active
> listening with each inactive member or inactive family . . . We assume this
> listening process is more likely to require six to ten hours, rather than two
> or three hours, if we are serious about getting beyond the veneer of excuses
> and discovering the basic reasons why this member is now inactive . . . We
> assume this process will probably require several visits, and it is unlikely
> to be accomplished in one or two visits. Frequently the first visit produces
> a series of excuses and guilt responses by the inactive member, the second
> visit releases a variety of hostile comments, and not until the third or
> fourth visit is the caller able to hear the basic reasons why this person is
> now inactive.[1]

As a means of equipping the ministry group members to be good
listeners, some time should be spent discussing the specifics of active
listening. Good conversation skills for ministry requires both verbal
and nonverbal skills. Verbal skills include: asking open-ended ques-

tions; focusing on feelings and problems; conveying understanding and acceptance of feelings and concerns; presenting oneself as an equal not an authority figure; expressing one's own feelings or personal experiences; and addressing direct questions and concerns.

Alfred Benjamin lists several verbal responses to be used in active listening, including silence, "mm-hm," restatement (saying the statement back to them verbatim), interpretation (rephrasing their statement in other words), encouragement, and assurance.[2] Each of these responses should be illustrated to the group by the leader.

Nonverbal responses in listening are very important in letting the speaker know one understands and is truly interested in what is being said. Several nonverbal responses should be illustrated for the group: affirmative head nods; calm, expressive facial movements; spontaneous eye movements and eye contact; looking at the person when they talk; gestures; relaxed posture, but not slouching; body positioned toward the person; and sitting close to the person.[3]

These responses and techniques can be developed and practiced during the role play interviews. The observer can help by giving the interviewer feedback on his listening skills.

Gently Probe for Information

Jill and Tom Baston were becoming discouraged with one of their reclamation assignments. Fred was a middle-aged gentleman, recently widowed. The Baston's were making their fifth visit to Fred's home. Up to this point, Fred had totally avoided the real issues of his inactivity.

After serving coffee to his newly found acquaintances, Fred soon began a monologue about his memories of his departed wife. They had once been very active in the church, both working together as teachers in the young adult department. As Fred continued with his unusually verbose remembrances, Jim asked, "Fred, why did you and Ruth ever get to be so inactive after all those years working with the Adult One Department?" Without a moment's pause, Fred responded, "I guess because all the old bunch is gone. They've either moved away or dropped out like me. Most of 'em have probably dropped out. It seems the younger folks in the class got unhappy because we had no class just for them. As a thirty-some-odd-year-old couple, it was a rude awakening to realize that the younger couples looked at us as middle-aged! So we just turned it over to them."

Instruct the ministry group that as the trust level builds in their relationship with the inactive member, they will be able to address the real problems of the member's inactivity. Offer caution against asking too many questions, but suggest they pick up on the cues from statements the member makes. This requires a great deal of sensitivity and dynamic listening.

Leave the "Door Open" for Future Visits

A couple of things need to be done before the conclusion of the visit in order to insure that the reclaimer can comfortably return at a future date to continue ministry.

Establish casual appointment. A casual appointment is one made impromptu, usually at the conclusion of the visit. The visitor may say something like, "I have really enjoyed talking with you, Mr. Smith. I would like to come by again for a visit, if you wouldn't mind. (Pause for response.) Perhaps in a couple of weeks about this same time. . . ." The group member would have to use his own discernment in making casual appointments.

Bring the pastor on visit. If the visitor feels it would be appropriate, the pastor might be brought in on a visit. If the pastor has been at the church only a short time, most of the inactive members will be unacquainted with him. The visitor should handle the situation something like this, "Mr. Smith, I feel it would be nice if Brother Jones could visit with us sometime. How about my seeing if he could come by with me sometime?"

Case Study

To gain more insight into the procedure for interviewing inactive members a case study is provided below with an evaluation. The situation of the study involves an inactive member, John, and a member of his church, Mike, who is serving in a reclamation project. John has been an inactive member for fourteen months. Mike is making his fourth contact with John: a visit in his home.

1. J: (answering the door) Hey, Mike, come on in.
2. M: Thanks, John. It's good to see you again. How's it going?
3. J: Fine. And you?
4. M: Great. The world been treating you pretty good?
5. J: Pretty good. It doesn't do any good to complain.
6. J: I know, sometimes it doesn't. But, then on the other hand sometimes . . .
7. J: You're probably going to ask me about church again.
8. M: Yes, I did want to talk about it. Do you mind?
9. J: Well, not really, I guess. *(Sigh.)*
10. M: Say, John, it seems to make you nervous to talk about it. Why is that?
11. J: Well, maybe, its just kinda everything that's going on right now. You know?
12. M: What is it, with your job?
13. J: Well, that too. Its just that I don't think I'll be going back to that church.
14. M: Why, John? Is something wrong?
15. J: Only with me, I guess. You see, its Jeannie . . .
16. M: Your wife?
17. J: Ex-wife. We're in divorce court this week. It's taken about a year to get to it.
18. M: I'm sorry, John. I didn't know it was coming up.
19. J: Yeah, its been pretty bad. She wants the house and the kids. I can see her getting the kids, but I won't get to see 'em except once a month. Looks like I'll be paying support and giving her the house, too. How am I supposed to get by?
20. M: You feel that the trial is turning out unfairly towards you. Sounds like you're pretty upset about it.
21. J: Well, how would you feel?
22. M: I honestly, don't know, John. I really don't know. I guess

it would make you feel pretty bad going to church with her there, not that she comes all that much.

23. J: I guess it has more to do with Debbie and Johnny than their mother. They go almost every Sunday. She sure wanted the judge to know that! You know, I just can't go to church feeling like that. Some people can . . . I can't.

24. M: You know, John, its your church, too.

25. J: Not really anymore, I guess she's taken that away from me, too. Not that I really went all that much. I just started going with her and the kids when things started getting bad between her and me. We felt it might help . . . you know, kind of a last ditch effort.

26. M: Did you ever talk with Pastor James? He's pretty good to talk to about stuff like that.

27. J: Oh, we tried. I think he was out of town one time, and I had a lot of overtime another time. We just never got together. I doubt if it would have helped much anyway. Doesn't really matter now, does it?

28. M: It might have made a difference. At least, you and Jeannie might be on better terms if you had talked it out with someone.

29. J: Maybe, so. But it would have only delayed the inevitable. She ran out on me. I didn't have that much to do with it. Well, I'm not saying I couldn't have done better, but that's no excuse for her. She's just like all them the hypocrites down there at that church . . . they dress up and go down there and act all righteous, when most of 'em are messin' 'round just like her. I just don't want no part of that. If that preacher down there knew what he was preachin' at he'd probably preach the Ten Commandments every Sunday.

30. M: He does preach them a lot.

31. J: That's good, maybe she'll hear it sometime.

32. M: Well, John, I know its rough for you right now. I just want you to know we'll be praying for you. Hang in there.

33. J: Yeah, thanks. I appreciate it. Hey, Mike, I feel like I

dumped all this on you tonight. I'm sorry. You didn't come over here to hear all my problems. I appreciate you stopping by, though.

34. M: Its all right, don't apologize. I feel honored that you would share something like that with me. It certainly helps me understand what's been going on. And I'll be able to pray for you more specifically now that I know just what kind of problems you've been facing.

35. J: That means a lot to me. Stop by some time.

36. M: Sure, I will. Keep me posted on how it goes.

37. J: Yeah, I will.

Evaluation

Compare the responses of Mike in the case study with the skills for good listening discussed above. Did Mike use good verbal skills and techniques? Let's review.

Actually, Mike handled the situation pretty well. It was a tense conversation. Obviously, Mike was able to establish a great amount of rapport with John in his previous visits, or the conversation would not have gotten so personal and Mike would not have been invited in so warmly. Although most of Mike's questions were close-ended, except for lines 2 and 10, he was able to focus the conversation on John's feelings and problems and convey understanding and acceptance (lines 22, 32, 34 and 36). Mike seemed to be taken aback by John's expressions of emotion and did not share his own feelings and experiences. In fact, John's emotional outburst put Mike on the defensive (lines 22, 28 and 30).

Except for lines 26 and 28, Mike was able to relate to John as an equal, without a critical standpoint. Line 20 is a good example of interpretation (rephrasing their statement in other words). Mike was able to offer words of encouragement in lines 24, 32 and 34.

The consistent and effective ways in which Mike was able to build a relationship with John is evident in line 33, when John expressed appreciation for Mike's willingness to hear his frustrations. This is another illustration of how the power of love supercedes technical skill and saved the day.

Find Them on the Telephone

An effective way of determining how receptive inactive members are to reclamation is a telephone canvass. In this way all the inactive members can be contacted in a relatively short period of time in a nonthreatening way. Group members are assigned a certain number of inactive members to call and are given the telephone numbers of these members.

It is helpful to first sit down with the group and go over the entire list of inactive members. Group members may be able to share pertinent information about the inactive members which would be helpful to the others. This is called the initial screening of the inactive members since several names will probably be removed from the list and not considered as candidates for ministry. These inactive members may have died, joined another church, or moved out of the area.

The ministry group should then be given about one week to contact the inactive members on their lists. The form given in Appendix B is recommended for this purpose and needs to be explained to the group. The questionnaire has seven questions designed to determine the receptivity of the inactive members. Each question is followed by a number of possible responses. The caller does not read these responses, but rather tries to fit the inactive member's response into one of these categories. The interviewer then writes the score corresponding to the response in the blank at the left. After the telephone conversation, the caller fills out the information at the bottom of the form and computes the Receptivity Scale by totaling the scores and dividing by seven.

After the telephone survey, all the scores for each inactive member can be tallied with the category information. Those inactive members receiving a receptivity rating of five or more should be considered as candidates for further ministry. This group of inactive members is called the target group.

You will notice that the caller asks the inactive member how he is doing three times at the beginning of the survey. It has been found that only after the third query will the person really begin to share how he is doing. Otherwise, the question is just a matter of courtesy.

Project Approach

The project approach is a way of doing reclamation ministry in a three-month emphasis. It is an intensive and encompassing method. It would be most useful in initiating reclamation in a church where very little emphasis has been placed on this ministry. It is a good way to start a reclamation ministry, so long as other ongoing approaches are established to maintain the ministry after the project is completed. See Appendix C for an outline of the project schedule.

The project begins with thorough planning. Ideally, the pastor should serve as the project leader and needs to have a good understanding of the various aspects of the project and be able to communicate this effectively to the participants. Set a date which allows for three months of uninterrupted work on reclamation.

Phase One: Enlistment and Orientation

Once all the plans are made and the date of the project has been set, you are ready to begin the first phase of the project: the enlistment and orientation of the group. This phase will require the first two weeks of the project. In week one the ministry group members are personally recruited. Six to twelve members would be an ideal number. These persons should have been contacted previously and indicated a willingness to serve. Special attention should be given to the qualifications of the participants as outlined above.

An open invitation may also be extended to the church through public announcement a week or two before the actual start of the project. This announcement serves a number of purposes. While certain persons may respond to the announcement who would not likely be good candidates for this ministry, the initial orientation and commitment will screen out most of the inappropriate ones. Such persons will probably realize this upon seeing the Ministry Agreement Form they will be expected to sign. Those unsure of their ability to fulfill the commitment should graciously be encouraged to wait for future opportunities.

Another purpose served by the public invitation for members to participate in the project is to inform the church. Its a way of saying, "We're doing something to reclaim our dropouts." Furthermore, the announcement would preclude any criticism of the ministry being closed to any except a select few or a clique. Besides, some members may have been overlooked in the recruitment who would serve well in the group!

The orientation session is held on week two of the project and includes a detailed presentation of the project idea and schedule. The Ministry Agreement Form is passed out and explained. At the conclusion of the session, members wishing to participate in the project are asked to sign the form and hand it in. In this way commitment and agreement is negotiated.

Phase Two: Preparation of the Ministry Group

By the third week of the project, the first of three teaching sessions takes place. Actually, every meeting of the group will involve teaching as the members grow in their awareness of reclamation ministry. Use the suggestions on training the group given above. The teaching outline given in Appendix A can be used as a workbook. Leave blanks and spaces in the outline for group members to fill in during the teaching sessions.

Four topics are discussed in the first session. First, members are asked to write out a definition of inactivity. These definitions are then compared with the one given in chapter seven.

Second, the group leader should present an analysis of the church as a way of demonstrating the need for ministry to inactive members. The analysis might include such facts as the number of active members and inactive members, the totals of membership over several years, and an evaluation of recent and current efforts at reclamation.

The third topic discussed in the first session is the strategy for the project. This will allow the group members to grasp the project as a whole. Two outlines of the strategy are given at the end of the teaching outline in Appendix A. The first outline is: *instruct, indentify, investigate,* and *interact.* The first aspect of the project is to *instruct* the ministry group via the teaching sessions. Next, the inactive members will be *identified* through group examination of the roll of church members. A telephone survey will be employed as a means of *investigating* the inactive members and determining their receptivity to future ministry. Finally, the group will *interact* with the inactive members as they make contacts.

The other strategy outline given is the A.C.T.I.V.E. acrostic. While this outline does not list the various phases of the ministry in chronological order, it will help the members to understand and remember the different elements involved in the project. The five elements are: *assess* the receptivity of inactive members and *categorize* them, *train* the ministry group, *identify* and *visit* the inactive members, and *evaluate* the results of the project.

The fourth topic presented in the first teaching session is the categories of inactivity. Since there will not be time enough to fully discuss the categories, the presentation will be carried over to the next teaching session. Categories of inactivity are discussed in chapter one.

The second teaching session will be held during week four. The discussion of the categories of inactivity will be concluded. This will probably require most of the session. Other aspects of inactivity presented in the book—psychological, spiritual and social—should also be presented in conjunction with the categories. In this way the members will receive an overview of the process of inactivity. It would be helpful to assign readings from appropriate sections of the book in anticipation of the sessions.

For Week	Read Chapter
2	Introduction
3	1,5,6
4	2,3,4
5	7

6   8
8   9

The concept of receptivity should be explained and discussed. Have the group brainstorm various ways the receptivity of the inactive members to ministry could be measured. It is important to have this discussion before preparing the telephone survey forms since the group may come up with new ideas to be incorporated into the survey.

The third teaching session is held in week five of the project. Methods for reclamation will be discussed using materials from chapter seven. In addition, role-play interviews, as previously discussed are conducted.

Phase Three: Discovery of Inactive Members

In the third phase of the project, weeks six and seven, the group will identify and survey the inactive members of the church. During the session in the sixth week, the group will discuss means of categorizing inactive members and determining their receptivity by using a telephone survey. In addition, the group will be given an overview of how the inactive members are to be contacted.

After the group discussion of contacting the inactive members, time will be spent in looking over the inactive member roll. This is called the initial screening of the target group because certain inactive members will be excluded at this point from reclamation ministry due to lack of information concerning their whereabouts or other factors. In addition, the total number of viable inactive members will be divided among the group, if possible, and assignments made for the telephone survey. A brief role play should be presented on how to conduct the survey.

The group will conduct the survey during the seventh week. At the conclusion of the week the group session will provide a time to discuss the results of the survey and assign specific inactive members to the group for ministry. Inactive members will be chosen for ministry on the basis of their receptivity and willingness to be contacted. Those inactive members with a receptivity rating of five or higher should be considered. As much as possible, group members should be allowed to choose their assignments.

Phase Four: Ministry to Inactive Members

Group members will make visits and other contacts with their assignments during weeks eight through eleven. Report sessions will also be held each week. During the sessions, group members may share their experiences and receive further instruction and encouragement.

During this phase data will be kept for each inactive member targeted. Group members will need to keep records of their contacts and report this information in the session. This data will be correlated and presented at the last group session in week twelve, after the group members have made their final visits. Statistical analyses should include the following: number of visits, telephone calls, and other contacts made to each inactive member by the group; tracking data on the activity of targeted members; and ratios of the numbers of contacts made to each member and that member's activity.

After the data is presented in the final session, the group can celebrate the results of reclaiming previously inactive members who are now showing signs of activity as well as discussing the need for ongoing ministry.

There are many resources available to churches wishing to do reclamation ministry. The Sunday School Board of the Southern Baptist Convention has produced an Equipping Center module entitled *Ingathering: Reclaiming Inactive Church Members* which is designed to lead a church in the project approach.[4] LEAD Consultants is another organization which provides resources for reclamation in the form of materials and workshops. John Savage, founder, is a minister in the United Methodist Church.[5]

Bible Study Organization

"Without a doubt, the program organization best equipped for tracking and contacting members as they become inactive in our church is the Sunday School (Bible study organization)." Pastor Jones was emphatic as he spoke up in the monthly church council meeting. This month's agenda centered on the growing problem of inactive membership. "It has already been demonstrated that the sooner intervention takes place in a member's inactivity the better," Jones continued. "Therefore, the key to an effective reclamation ministry would be tracking. Weekly attendance records need to be maintained for each church member. Our Sunday School classes already keep detailed attendance records, and some are good in contacting their absentees."

Cynthia Cox, Faith Church's new Sunday School director, picked up the pastor's lead, "Since we started keeping Sunday School attendance records on computer, the amount of manpower needed each Sunday morning for record keeping has been reduced greatly while increasing the capacity for tracking members' attendance. Our new software allows us to tally the members' overall attendance records to date with each week's entries, and print an updated record form to be used each week in lieu of the old card file."

"How does the computer help us spot absentees?" queried Jack Parker, outreach director. "Members who have been absent for two Sundays in a row are indicated on the record sheet for the upcoming Sunday," Cynthia answered. "This makes it easy to spot persons who are dropping out."[6]

"Looks like we'll need someone in each Sunday School class, as an outreach leader, with the responsibility of contacting members who have been absent. Also, these workers will need to be trained in the process of reclamation ministry," Jack concluded.

Deacon Ministry

Baker Hill United Community Church employs another approach for reclaiming with great potential through the deacon ministry of the church. Monthly deacons meetings serve as an ideal time frame for member evaluation. A portion of each meeting is designated for the review and discussion of member inactivity. Baker Hill's approach to reclamation ministry would involve the following elements.

Training

Deacons are trained in the project ministry in a workshop series on Saturdays, or even by setting aside a part of each meeting for training. Ideally, deacons' retreats for this purpose are planned one a year, if possible. In the retreat setting, the entire training process is completed at one time.

Tracking

Again, tracking is a crucial aspect of reclamation. In addition to Sunday School attendance, records are kept on worship attendance. A deacon sub-committee was formed to monitor worship attendance. I have used this approach and found it to work well if consistently maintained. A deacon, or usher, is given an attendance roll with a printed list of all active members. At each service, this person stands in the rear of the auditorium and checks off the members who were present during that service. It was also surprising how many members the deacons did not know. Their getting to know each active member by name was an added benefit. Other methods for tabulating worship attendance were discussed in the previous chapter.

In the monthly deacons meeting, attendance information is shared for members discovered to be absent for more than a certain number of weeks, or showing a decrease in attendance. The church computer has been utilized to quickly tally this information.

Church members may react to keeping records for worship attendance. Although churches of many denominations do this successfully, worship attendance records are not usually kept in some churches. Attendance would need to be recorded discreetly in a manner acceptable to the congregation.

Assignment and Contact

As members who need reclamation are discovered, assignments are made to a specific deacon for contact. Deacons have assignments for a specified geographical area in which the member lives. Some churches give membership assignments through a plan of deacon family ministry. In the latter case, deacons would assume responsibility for contacting their assigned families when reclamation was needed.

At each meeting, reports of contacts are shared to assure accountability and ongoing learning.

Accountability

One drawback in this approach has to do with accountability. It is conceivable that a member could be inactive for three to four weeks before assignment for contact was made in the regular monthly meetings. Contacts by the deacons might not be made until just before the next monthly meeting, when a report would have to be given. Consequently, a member could be inactive for seven to eight weeks before a contact was made. This time period is nearing the outer limits of the waiting period inactive members have before reinvesting their energies in other pursuits and becoming extremely hard to reclaim.

The Baker Hill Church has solved this problem by asking that the deacon contact be made within the week of the monthly meetings. This assures the greatest possible success in reclamation. The reclamation sub-committee chairman or the deacon chairman contacts the deacons a week after the monthly meeting to see that contacts had been made.

Evangelism/Discipleship Programs

Many churches have ongoing programs of evangelism and discipleship. Since the follow-up, or discipleship, portion of such ministries is strong, it could be effective in reclamation as well. In addition to assigning prospects to the visiting teams each week, inactive members could be assigned. The visitation teams would contact the person and use their follow-up procedures and materials.

The strengths of this type of approach would be numerous. First, evangelism/discipleship programs are a preventative to inactivity. No doubt, one of the contributing factors to the number of inactive members in churches is a lack of discipleship. By discipling members as they are reached by the church, a significant improvement of the inactive situation should be realized over time.

Second, such programs are already structured for contacting. The only real difference, then, would be in adding the inactive members as assignments. After all, evangelism without concomitant discipleship is irresponsible and discipleship without evangelism is sterile. Furthermore, is not the existence of inactive members a symptom of the need for discipleship?

The third strenth of this approach is that the materials of evangelism/discipleship programs are well suited for reclamation. Perhaps if the inactive members had been discipled to begin with, they would not have become inactive. It could be a very positive ministry of spiritual development for inactive members to go through a discipleship program as provided by these ministries.

Fourth, since timing is crucial in reclamation, discipleship programs would be an asset to reclamation as visits are made on a weekly basis. Some evangelism/discipleship programs, however, function for only eight months a year, which would leave four months of ministry to be done through another organization.

Fifth, in a church where the deacon ministry or Bible study outreach is weak, evangelism/discipleship programs could serve as the "front line" of the reclamation ministry. Even in the presence of other reclamation programs, such a ministry would provide support for reclamation of members overlooked by other organizations.

A sixth strength of this approach is that assignments are made to specific individuals and teams for follow-up. This builds responsibility and accountability into the program as well as fostering permanent relationships.

Missions Organizations

The men's and women's missions organizations of a church could also be utilized in the ministry of reclamation. Many missions organizations hold monthly meetings which, like deacons meetings, could involve discovery and assignment of inactive members for organization members to contact. Training could be done in the context of the organization as well. Although reclamation may not relate directly to the purpose of such organizations, these may serve a valuable purpose in the absence of any other organization doing reclamation ministry. In addition, reclamation, as a ministry, could transform many of these organizations from a social organization to a ministry action group while providing yet another small group for the inclusion of members in the fellowship of the church. (See chapter 4.)

Repeat the Project Periodically

The project approach could be repeated on a periodic basis, for example, once or twice a year. While such an approach would not provide the needed ongoing ministry on a weekly or monthly basis throughout the year, it certainly would be a valuable tool in addition to, or in the absence of, other approaches.

One asset of the project approach is its thoroughness. Though members may not necessarily be ministered to as they become inactive, the project would reach the entire group of inactive members in the church who could be contacted.

Another asset of repeating the project is the possibility of using the same ministry group in future ministry projects. This would shorten the time span of the project by eliminating much of the training time. Indeed, further training could be done to sharpen the skills of the project group and to help them learn greater ways of coping with the anxieties experienced.

In addition, project members could be used as leaders of other ministry groups. This approach does hold the possibility of an ongoing ministry. A separate project group could operate each month, or quarter, thus maintaining a continuous tracking, surveying, and ministry to inactive members.

Care would need to be taken, if the project were repeated, in using the telephone survey. It would be redundant and ineffective to use the same survey for a person who was being reclaimed a second time. An ongoing ministry, preferably by the initial ministry team, should be given to such repeat inactive members.

Another Committee

Most churches have committees for every other conceivable need, why not a reclamation committee? Such a committee would be responsible for developing and maintaining the total reclamation ministry of the church and coordinating it with the ministry organizations and the pastor.

Such a committee, if large enough, could be divided into subcommittees for tracking, surveying, and contacting inactive members. This approach would provide an ongoing ministry as well as a ministry group inclusive of all structures in the church. Leaders of the various program organizations could even be made ex-officio members of the reclamation committee, assuring broad representation.

Paired Members

As another means of preventing inactivity, a paired members approach could be used, pairing a trained volunteer member with a new member. This approach could even be used for members who have become inactive. Although, from the inactive member's perspective, this approach would be little different from the group approach (since assignments to the group members are on a one-to-one basis), it would have the effect of providing a long-term relationship with another member as a support mechanism. It has been found that if inactive members had someone to undergird them during a crisis time and serve to mobilize the ministry of the church, they would not have become inactive.

One way to implement such a program would be to assign an encourager member to an inactive member immediately upon his discovery to be inactive, or to a new member upon uniting with the church. This assignment could be made by the pastor from a pool of volunteers who have been trained for this purpose.[7]

Two resources available for this type of ministry are the New Christian Encourager Plan and the booklet *One in the Bond of Love* by Donald Whitehouse.[8]

Cell Groups

A form of ministry fellowship in widespread use today is the cell group concept. Simply stated, cell groups are small groups wherein members share their time, experiences, and needs on a weekly basis. Cell groups even become a channel for ministry activities.

If your church has a network of cell groups in operation (these can even be Bible study groups), your problem of inactive members has probably already been impacted significantly. Cell groups are a means for the church to directly address the intimacy and ministry needs of members. A good resource for the development of cell groups in the church is the TOUCH Ministries approach, which includes a church-based seminar.[9]

Notes

[1]Lyle E. Schaller, *Assimilating New Members* (Nashville: Abingdon, 1978), p. 118.

[2]Alfred Benjamin, *The Helping Interview* (Dallas: Houghton Mifflin Company, 1969), pp. 110-128.

[3]Steven J. Danish and Allen L Hauer, *Helping Skills* (New York: Human Sciences Press, 1977), p. 85.

[4]Information about this module is available by contacting the Sunday School Board of the S.B.C., Nashville, TN 37234.

[5]For a list of publications and workshops offered by LEAD Consultants write: LEAD Consultants, Inc., P.O. Box 311, Pittsford, New York 14534.

[6]One fairly inexpensive program available, which the author helped design, is the Softworks Church Data System. For information on the SCDS program (available on IBM and Victor format) write: Softworks, 5041 Glade St., Fort Worth, TX 76114.

[7]For a succinct and helpful discussion of what some churches term a "Barnabas" ministry, see Charles Mylander, *Secrets For Growing Churches* (Harper and Row: San Francisco, 1979), pp. 71ff.

[8]Materials for both of these resources are available from the Sunday School Board of the S.B.C., 127 Ninth Avenue, North, Nashville, TN 37234.

[9]For materials and services offered by TOUCH Ministries write: TOUCH Ministries, Inc., Box 19888, Houston, TX 77224.

Appendix A

Training Outline

I. The Definition of Inactivity
"An 'inactive church member' is a resident member of the church who has ceased to participate in the life and work of the church as evidenced by a lack of attendance and financial support or who has shown a marked decrease in such participation to the point that this participation is minimal."

II. The Need for Ministry to Inactive Members
The number of resident members
The number of active members
The number of inactive members

III. The Process of Inactivity
A. The Anxiety-Provoking Event
1. 90 percent can recall an event or series of events that led to their inactivity.
2. Forms of Anxiety
   a. Reality
   b. Neurotic
   c. Moral
   d. Existential
   These impact upon the following categories.
3. Categories of "Reasons" for Inactivity
   a. Conflict

116

       (1) With pastor, perhaps some disagreement

       (2) With another church member, perhaps resulting in loss of important friendship

       (3) With someone beyond membership, usually another family member

       (4) Theological issues

       (5) Financial issues (money represents values and power), financial preoccupation of church leadership.

       (6) Those who just can't tolerate conflict (fall out)

   b. Unmet Expectations

       (1) Disappointment with pastoral relationship

       (2) Social satisfactions

       (3) Worship

       (4) Overworked/burned out (expectations of themselves and God)

   c. Lack of Affinity

       (1) Homogeneous principle

       (2) Loss of important friendships

       (3) Disappointment with pastoral role

       (4) Need for personal religious independence

       (5) Boredom, no relationship to member's own goals and values

   d. Inability to relate

       (1) "Church hoppers"

       (2) Special variety of angry/withdrawn

B. Coping with the Anxiety

  1. "In flight"

  2. Conversion to anger

  3. "Cries for help" (initial ways of letting you know)

   a. Wayne Oates, "Their anger and resentment are really shrieks of pain upon having been severely mistreated, neglected, ignored, excluded, and denigrated."

   b. Direct:Angry/outspoken

   c. Indirect

       (1) Subtle comments

          (2) Angry/depressed

          (3) Angry/manipulative

          (4) Angry/withdrawn

    4. Anxiety Heightened

       a. No response to initial cries

         (1) Indirect: not noticed

         (2) Direct: creates distance, reaction

       b. Behavioral changes over 6-8 week period (sequence of dropping out of these involvements)

         (1) Worship

         (2) Committees, other groups

         (3) Giving

    5. The Pathology of Inactivity

       a. How to cope with long-term anxiety?

       b. Spiritual implications

IV. Spiritual Dimensions

  A. The Kingdom questions

  B. Theological issues

 V. Sociological Factors

  A. Facilities

  B. Services

  C. Fellowship

  D. Intimacy

  E. Leadership

VI. The Strategy of Ministry

  A. Instruct ministry group

  B. Identify inactive members

  C. Investigate inactive members

  D. Interact with inactive members

  E. A.C.T.I.V.E. (Assess—Categorize—Train—Identify—Visit—Evaluate)

Appendix B

Telephone Survey Form

Name_____ Phone _____

_____ "This is _____, from (name of church), and I'm helping to take a survey of our members for a church project. How are you? Would you mind talking with me a moment about our church and answering a few questions?" no (1) guess so (5) yes (10)

"Has everything been going well for you?"

1. "Would you say things have been going 'really great' (1), 'so-so' (5), or 'terrible' (10)"

_____
_____
_____

_____ 2. "Have there been any changes in your life lately? very little (1), some change (5), a great deal of change (10)"

_____
_____
_____

_____ 3. "How do you *feel* about the church? negative (1) indifferent (5) positive (10)"

_____
_____
_____

4. "This is a yes-no question. Can you think of some specific event that

119

led to your being less active in the church now than you used to be? Circle:
no yes

5. If yes, "Would you mind sharing that with me?"

_____ Conflict

_____ Pastor _____

_____ Church member _____

_____ Nonmember (family, etc) _____

_____ Theological _____

_____ Financial _____

_____ _____

_____ Unmet expectations

_____ Pastor _____

_____ Social _____

_____ Worship _____

_____ Burned out _____

_____ _____

_____ Lack of affinity

_____ Loss of friends _____

_____ Pastor _____

_____ Bored _____

_____ _____

_____ Inability to relate _____

_____

_____

_____

_____ 6. "How near are you to becoming more active in our church? far (1)
not near (5) very near (10)"

_____

_____ 7. "Would you be willing for a member of our church to talk with you
further about these things?" no (1) unsure (5) yes (10)

Talk to other inactive members in household.

Interviewer

Name _____

_____ Anxiety of inactive member: high (1) moderate (5) low (10)

_____ Easy to talk to: no (1) yes (10)

Category (Question 5) _____

Other comments _____

_____

_____

_____

Total Score (add scores of all questions,   _____
                          including anxiety and easy to talk to)

Divide Total Score by 7 (=Receptivity Scale)   _____

Appendix C

Project Schedule Outline

I. Enlistment and Orientation
  A. Week One: Enlistment of Ministry Group Members
  B. Week Two: Orientation Session
II. Preparation of the Ministry Group: Teaching Sessions
  A. Week Three: Teaching Session One
    1. The definition of inactivity
    2. The need for ministry to inactive members
    3. The strategy for the project
    4. The categories of inactivity (part one)
  B. Week Four: Teaching Session Two
    1. The categories of inactivity (part two)
    2. Levels of receptivity
  C. Week Five: Teaching Session Three
    1. Methodologies for reclaiming inactive members
    2. Role play interviews
III. Discovery of Inactive Members
  A. Week Six: Identifying Inactive Members
    1. Group discussion
      a. Means of categorizing inactive members
      b. Means of determining receptivity
      c. Means of reclaiming inactive members
    2. Initial screening of target group

B. Week Seven: Phone Canvass of Inactive Members
  1. Phone Calls to target group by ministry group
  2. Group discussion of canvass results
     a. Correlate results of canvass
     b. Further screening of target group
     c. Assignment of inactive members group members

IV. Ministry to Inactive Members
  A. Weeks Eight through Eleven: Visitation to Inactive Members
    1. Group members visit assignments
    2. Report sessions each week
  B. Week Twelve: Final Visitation and Evaluation
    1. Final visits to assignments
    2. Final report session and evaluation

Bibliography

Books

Bagby, Daniel G. *Understanding Anger in the Church*. Nashville: Broadman Press, 1979.

Bangham, William. *Journey into Small Groups*. 1548 Poplar Avenue, Memphis, TN 38104: Brotherhood Commission of the SBC, 1974.

Benjamin, Alfred. *The Helping Interview*. Dallas: Houghton Mifflin Company, 1974.

Bennett, Thomas R. II. *The Leader and the Process of Change*. New York: Association Press, 1962.

Biersdorf, John E. *Hunger for Experience*. New York: The Seabury Press, 1975.

Bonhoeffer, Dietrich. *Life Together*. New York: Harper and Row, 1954.

Booher, Dianna Daniels. *Getting Along With People Who Don't Get Along*. Nashville: Broadman Press, 1984.

Bow, Russell. *The Integrity of Church Membership*. Waco: Word Books, 1968.

Cole, W. Douglas. *When Families Hurt*. Nashville: Broadman Press, 1979.

Dale, Robert D. *Growing a Loving Church*. Nashville: Convention Press, 1974.

Danish, Stephen J. and Hauer, Allen L. *Helping Skills: A Basic Training Program*. New York: Human Science Press, 1977.

Dudley, Carl S. *Where Have All Our People Gone?* New York: The Pilgrim Press, 1979.

Frankl, Viktor E. *Man's Search for Meaning.* New York: Pocket Books, 1973.

Gibble, Jay E. *Reaching Out to the Missing Ones.* Elgin: The Brethren Press, 1981.

Gray, L. Charles. *Reaching the Drop Out Church Member.* New York: The Program Agency of the United Presbyterian Church in the U.S.A., 1982.

Greenfield, Guy. *We Need Each Other.* Grand Rapids: Baker Book House, 1984.

Hauch, Paul A. *Overcoming Frustration and Anger.* Philadelphia: Westminster Press, 1974.

Hoehn, Richard A. *Up from Apathy.* Nashville: Abingdon Press, 1983.

Howe, Reuel L. *The Miracle of Dialogue.* New York: The Seabury Press, 1963.

Hyer, Marjorie. *The Empty Pew.* Pittsford: LEAD Consultants, Inc., 1979.

Killinger, John. *Christ in the Seasons of Ministry.* Waco: Word Books, 1981.

Koteskey, Ronald L. *General Psychology for Christian Counselors.* Nashville: Abingdon Press, 1983.

Krahn, John H. *Reaching the Inactive Member.* Lima: The C.S.S. Publishing Company, Inc., 1982.

Leas, Speed B. *Leadership and Conflict.* Nashville: Abingdon Press, 1982.

Lewin, Kurt. *Field Theory in Social Science.* New York: Harper and Brothers Publishers, 1951.

_____. *Resolving Social Conflicts.* New York: Harper and Brothers Publishers, 1948.

Madden, Myron C. *The Power to Bless.* Nashville: Broadman Press, 1970.

McSwain, Larry L., and Treadwell, William C. *Conflict Ministry in the Church.* Nashville: Broadman Press, 1981.

Minirth, Frank B., and Meier, Paul D. *Happiness Is a Choice.* Grand Rapids: Baker Book House, 1978.

Mylander, Charles. *Secrets for Growing Churches.* San Francisco: Harper and Row, 1979.

Nouwen, Henri J.M.. *The Wounded Healer.* Garden City: Doubleday and Company, Inc., 1972.

Rothauge, Arlin J. *Sizing Up a Congregation.* Seabury Professional Services, 1984.

Savage, John S. *The Apathetic and Bored Church Member.* Pittsford: LEAD Consultants, Inc., 1976.

Schaller, Lyle E. *Assimilating New Members.* Nashville: Abingdon Press, 1979.

——————. *Activating the Passive Church.* Nashvile: Abingdon Press, 1981.

Schmidt, Paul F. *Coping with Difficult People.* Philadelphia: Westminster Press, 1980.

Whitehouse, Donald S., *One in the Bond of Love,* a work-book for new christians. 127 Ninth Avenue, North, Nashville, TN 37234: The Sunday School Board of the SBC, 1987.

Periodicals and Journals

Alsup, John E. "The Doctrine of Church Membership and Discipline." *Austin Seminary Bulletin* 95 (October 1979): 5-10.

Bass, James D. "Politics in the Church." *Search* (Fall 1982): 29-31.

Brown, Harold Glen. "How to Avoid Tearing Apart Your Church." *The Christian Ministry* 12 (September 1981): 31-33.

——————. "Trying to Save an Antagonist." *The Christian Ministry* 14 (July 1983): 25-26.

Frykholm, Robert A. "A Relational Theology of the Laity." *The Iliff Review* 37 (Fall 1980): 13-25.

Hansen, Richard R. "The Sound of Clashing Expectations." *Leadership* (Summer 1984): 78-83.

Hedges, Barbara J. "Recruiting and Training Volunteers." *Church Administration,* March 1983, pp. 14-18.

Hutcheson, Richard G., Jr. "Dealing with Dissidents." *The Christian Ministry* 13 (November 1982): 16-18.

Jones, Mark S. "A Neglected Ministry, Reclaiming." *The Baptist Program,* October 1984, pp. 7-8.

Justice, William G. "The Power of Guilt and Forgiveness." *Church Administration,* February 1982, pp. 13-14.

Leas, Speed. "Conflict in the Parish: How Bad Is It?" *Word and World* 4 (Spring 1984): 182-191.

Muck, Terry C. "Training Volunteers: A Leadership Survey." *Leadership*
(Summer 1982): 40-48.

Ortland, Raymond C. "Priorities for the Local Church." *Bibliotheca Sacra*
138 (January-March 1981): 3-12.

——————. "The First Business of God's People." *Bibliotheca Sacra* 138
(April-June 1981): 99-107.

——————. "Being the People of God Together." *Bibliotheca Sacra* 138
(July-September 1981): 195-202.

——————. "Sharing God's Concern for the World." *Bibliotheca Sacra*
138 (October-December 1981): 291-301.

Outler, Albert C. "Power and Grace." *Perkins Journal* (Fall 1984): 20-27.

Taylor, Dan. "The Mid-Life Transition and Middle Age: Implications for
Churches." *Search* (Spring 1981): 26-33.

Smith, Fred. "The Manipulation Game." *Leadership* (Fall 1985): 110-116.

Zens, Jon. "Building Up The Body—One Man or One Another?" *Baptist
Reformation Review* 10 (Second Quarter 1981): 10-33.

Tape Recordings

Savage, John S. *The Apathetic and Bored Church Member*. Pittsford: LEAD
Consultants, Inc., 1976.